When The Sun Goes Down And The Drip Goes Up

Gill Bucklitsch

authorHOUSE®

AuthorHouse™ UK Ltd.
500 Avebury Boulevard
Central Milton Keynes, MK9 2BE
www.authorhouse.co.uk
Phone: 08001974150

© 2009 Gill Bucklitsch. All rights reserved.

No part of this book may be reproduced, stored in a retrieval system, or transmitted by any means without the written permission of the author.

First published by AuthorHouse 10/6/2009

ISBN: 978-1-4490-3161-9 (sc)

This book is printed on acid-free paper.

Acknowledgements

This book is dedicated first of all to a special friend who relentlessly encouraged me to complete it.

Also to other real friends Jenny, Helen, Shellie, Suzanne and Elaine, amongst others, who congratulated me on my achievement and I know will enjoy not only buying it but reading it too.

To all my friends and companions who worked with me in the numerous hospitals in Mallorca and Tenerife. Thanks go to all the doctors who unfailingly answered my questions especially during the very busy summer months.

Thanks go to my brother Ian, my father and Ruth who have watched and helped me from up above.

And to Ross who showed me how passionate I was about what I had written.

Contents

Chapter 1 Change Of Accommodation	1
Chapter Two Bad Indigestion	4
Chapter Three Wrong Time, Wrong Place	14
Chapter Four " I′Ve Got An Insurance"	24
Chapter Five Law And Order	35
Chapter Six "Grandad′S On Holiday"	41
Chapter Seven An Unwelcome Break	48
Chapter Eight "I Didn't Think It Was That Serious"	55
Chapter Nine No Breathing Problems	66
Chapter Ten Little One′S Problems	75
Chapter Eleven A Wee Drop Too Much	85
Chapter 12 Sun, Sea And A&E	97

Chapter 1

Change of Accommodation

"Oh no!" exclaimed Betty. "I can't stay in hospital overnight! I'm on holiday. It will spoil it for everyone else!" She had been brought in just an hour ago in an emergency ambulance. Tests proved beyond doubt that she had just had a heart attack. But she wasn't having any of it. A hospital stay was not what she had planned for the holiday and this was, after all, a foreign country.

I work as an Interpreter, part of the welfare team in a small Spanish hospital on the island of Majorca. We will call it St Mero in Sta Gracia. Now Sta Gracia is a very pretty town of about 25,000 people but it's population more than doubles in the holiday months as holiday makers come from all over Europe to lie on the beaches and walk in the mountains. In addition it has got more than it's fair share of expatriates, retiring to enjoy the sun. Some of these tourists get holidays that they will always remember and not always because of the weather.

I want to tell some of their stories. There is a reason. There is a message here. Some people blandly believe they have "holiday insurance that covers everything". It doesn't. Equally, some people seem to believe that just because they are on holiday and carefree, nothing dangerous can happen to them. Or indeed that they can get seriously ill. Yet, having been involved with such people for over a decade, explaining to them what the doctors are saying when they can't speak a word of Spanish, believe me, their lives can be changed for the worse in a minute. And the worst of it is that it could often be so easily avoided.

Betty was one of these cases and we saved her life. She had woken up with "heavy pain" in her chest, swiftly followed by "another going down my left arm". As so often happens, her husband encouraged her to go back to sleep after giving her a massage and some painkillers, "Don't worry. We'll see how it is in the morning then we'll see a doctor if you want". She woke again after an hour in considerably more pain. They called a doctor and she was whisked into our hospital, ambulance sirens blaring.

Like many others, there was no warning. She had never been diagnosed with anything. In the following chapters, there are plenty of cases like Betty who was so reluctant to stay overnight. We had talked to her husband and managed to persuade him of the danger she would be in if she simply walked out. Fortunately she changed her mind. "Well alright then, but only for one night!" She left us ten days later by ambulance with a Medical Escort. She was lucky.

Some of these cases are sad and sometimes very distressing. But others are also plain straight funny. And there are tales of unexpected backing by family, friends, medical staff, volunteers and sometimes complete strangers. There is anger too at the stupidity of the youngsters and some not so young away for a good time. Stories of indifference as a friend is taken to hospital with both legs broken, after falling off a stage that was "a lot higher than we first thought!"

There is pain both physical and emotional here, caused by upsets and inconvenient illnesses. But there is affection and laughter too as "patients" begin to admit that there is nothing else they can do as "the sun goes down and the drip goes up". All these cases are true, but names have been changed. If you recognise your own experience let us hope we meet again in better circumstances.

Chapter two
BAD INDIGESTION

One of the worst scenarios, while on holiday is to be told that you have had a heart attack. Just as bad for some could be a sudden ´stroke ´.It happens so often. Without warning on numerous occasions. Holiday makers hardly ever heed the obvious signs. They may never have been told why they are taking certain medication. Bad indigestion and heartburn is the most frequent interpretation for cardiac related conditions. They take a ´Rennies¨ and hope it will go away!! My role as interpreter involves obtaining answers for the treating doctor. I remember having to ask a patient if they had high blood pressure"Oh no. I haven't got that"He stated! "So why are you taking blood pressure tablets "I inquired. His reply was "I don't have high blood pressure because I take those tablets everyday "

I understand the reasoning here but why doesn't the GP explain fully? Maybe he did! And wasn't taken seriously! Or the explanation was misinterpreted. It is a statement on which Insurance companies base their decisions to cover a case. Read on and take heed. Share with me some similar situations which have come my way.

Betty was so like many other cases we have dealt with. Lily was another such sudden attack. She arrived on holiday after what she described as "a funny sort of flight "And told us "I've never felt better" Her appearance was almost normal except for her healthy red cheeks. Poor soul she hadn't even got to the beach. The ambulance arrived from the East coast. And that was some forty minutes away. Her husband, who was only just coping, was worried about" getting back for dinner". This didn't happen of course. He was there for breakfast though to meet his son who flew out immediately.

Lily's case was dealt with and diagnosed very quickly. She had an obstruction and this was giving her slight Angina attacks. Undetected before! We laughed together during her stay in hospital as she learnt more about her near escape. She listened to our doctors and did all they told her. An Angiogram was indicated, a tube with a camera fed through her groin up to her heart. The diagnosis showed exactly the position of the problem. Her Insurance Company didn't want to believe she was as bad as our doctors were saying. So eventually, they made their decision. The countless phone calls from her son, who was prepared "to come out fighting as it's my Mum we're talking about" were passed over. They wanted her to be flown home and have treatment in the Uk. But our treating doctors refused to sign a fit to fly. The insurance company, therefore, has to take full responsibility when they go against the treating doctor's recommendation.

Insurance Companies are not on the spot and are really talking about numbers. The patient is a person lying in front of us and needs treating. The family is so vulnerable and inclined to agree with whatever the

Insurance Company dishes out. Not always in the patients interest, might I add! Lovely Lily, because she was such a brave lady and a joy to talk to, was escorted home by an Insurance Company doctor without an Angiogram and admitted into hospital in the Uk. She was put on a waiting list. Even today she may not even have had her ´Angiogram´ yet.

Another case, who we shall call Terry White, was swimming in the pool and exercising. This being a daily habit he had practised for years. The doctor examining him was told that out of the blue "I felt cramp in my left arm and a pain going around to my back" Lucky and very sensible man who told his friends to "call the doc" His treatment included an emergency Angiogram as a matter of life or death. He was whisked away to our sister hospital across the island to return the next day with three stents in place! And he was so grateful. Five days later I couldn't contain him in his room and found him in all different parts of the hospital "gently exercising. It's what the doctor ordered" was the answer I got. He really was being very enthusiastic but rightly so.

We had a bit of a set to! On being discharged he loudly told me that we

had failed to give him his tests back. Now I say loudly because he actually shouted at me. I went in search of the wretched CD! It really is so important that he should show it to his own doctor on his return home. And I was a bit annoyed when I found out that the CD was already in his care. He had ´pocketed´ it during the ambulance drive back to us after his stent inserts.

The CD was of his Angiogram and invariably makes a wonderful evening's entertainment for the patient and their family. This really does happen as several patients have often told me. Terry was a nice man, also very attractive and we parted good friends. He revisited us three months later and made a very appreciable monetary gift to the hospital and staff. The welfare team was given lots of chocolates too. "You all saved my life and what more can I say "He commented.

Being part of a team makes dealing with problems easier. We get together and chew over the days events. Pooling our ideas can be fun too. So nice to return after a couple of days off to find that my colleagues have done their best to inform the patient and advise as well as I would. Many times patients and their families show their gratitude with tasty goodies. They really are so overwhelmed that we helped to put them on the road to recovery. The holiday is greatly appreciated after such an experience.

John was a wonderful ballroom dancer and had been dancing the night away to the hotel's resident band when disaster struck." He just fainted away in my arms to the Cha, Cha beat" his wife for fifty years told us. Regaining consciousness in the ambulance while hurtling along the country roads, he wanted to turn around "I didn't get to do my quickstep" He complained. As he had fainted he was a suspected stroke sufferer. Now can you imagine having to go through all the tests including a brain scan, to be repeated after forty eight hours? How can a 'patient' who feels so much better have the tolerance to wait this time? Remember all these people are desperately wanting to continue their holiday. John had a history of a heart flutter so our docotor couldn't sign him out until this had been investigated. In the end he understood as he admitted that his own GP had "found something suspicious"

How disturbing it was when John and his wife spent five days waiting for the Cardiologist to get everything done. He walked up and down the corridors all day. I had to take different routes to avoid the same question." What time is the Cardiologist coming?" Family members sometimes pour oil on troubled waters. Their opinion is reversed when they see "Mum and Dad get better" How nice for the patient to return to the Uk with a clean bill of health and up to date medical report for their own GP. "That'll show him" John announce with pride on his discharge. He had to get back to his hotel as his son was due to depart on the first available flight. Just as soon as he got mum and Dad settled, was their son's intention. He wanted to be sure that John would be cautious for the remainder of the holiday. Good for you John. And thanks for listening!

Must tell you about Jeremy. He appeared to be on the way out. His partner was distressed and Jeremy frightened!. But he sent her home on their original flight that same day!. Margaret left in tears, as indeed they both were. She pressed his passport into my pocket and tearfully stressed " I love him so much, please send him home safely" Now Jeremy made a miraculous recovery except for the slight reactions he was getting from his brain. The doctor examined him for a brain tumour. Then ruled out epilepsy too. The doctors told me they were convinced he'd had a transitory stroke. Not as serious as a ´ brain haemorrhage! ´ Nevertheless he still had to be ´declared fit to fly ´In between the usual numerous calls to his Insurance Company, we kept Margaret reasonably satisfied on the end of the phone. Jeremy spent a lot of time "In the fresh air "I wasn't aware till the last day that his idea of fresh air meant a regular walk down to the local beach! He did turn a rather dark shade of brown whilst with us as an in patient. "You do look well Jeremy "commented most of the other patients. As my role involves being a go between I mustn't judge or interfere. The time came to think about sending him home. It was Friday and the doctors were happy with him. They went off duty but two hours later we were informed that a medical escort was on his way to take him home.

When a patient has had any form of a stroke he has to have a fit to fly signed by the treating doctor. This hadn't been done! And it was the weekend. Jeremy's repatriation with the nurse was cancelled. His ´ tan deepened ´ and he left us finally three days later with the same male nurse, Hugo, who returned for him. Hugo was happy to get another trip out here so soon. He was stunned by Jeremy's tan too. Jeremy admitted everything to us on his last day and advised us ´ how to get a good tan´. Needless to say we informed the other patients this really wasn't general practice. I had to chuckle to myself at the way he had bent the rules. I give him full marks for secrecy. We had never 'rumbled him'. Margaret wasn't too happy though.

Sharing these anecdotes makes our day bearable. Situations arise that are difficult to get through. How can you sit down to plan a day with the incredibly variable situations we find ourselves involved in? The sad, the stressing, the odd, the complicated, the outrageous and of course the plain straight funny. Thinking after of how we manage to dovetail it all in is fascinating. Being givers and helpers is our code in this job. Body language has never been so significant and important.

Eric Winston had such wonderful continual family support. He was 74 and his wife 72. Their holiday was taken with all his family. Two sons and two daughters. What lovely folk! Eric collapsed on his son's boat while fishing close to the port. He arrived at the hospital in record time to be told he was having a massive heart attack. It was touch and go for three days. He pulled through. Then the trouble started. He was declined by the insurance company! He hadn't declared ´ some small condition´. A lesson to be learnt! By the time the doctors had finally got him stabilised an air ambulance had been organised by the family as requested by the Intensive Care Doctor.

The family were all there to see Mum and Dad leave together. I just had to be close at hand too although it was midnight. Another long but satisfying day for me. And I managed a drink with them all before leaving the hospital. That experience taught us all something about support and loyalty. They contacted our team shortly after to say "an enormous thank you "to all our staff. Eric recuperated in record time. To then return for another holiday with the boat! And he got adequate insurance cover! Sensible man and his family.

Not so lucky was Barbara Brown, her brain haemorrhage caused a lot of damage and paralysis. Her support around her was her daughter and family. I went to visit her on her first day in intensive care. And her distress was so apparent. When her funny turn had happened she told us she had been "playing snap with the grandchildren" The game was never finished. She tearfully begged us. "Please don't let them see me like this". Not easy to keep loved ones at bay! They loved their grandmother so much. By lunchtime disaster struck twice! We had to admit her son in law with gastroenteritis. The family divided their visits between the intensive care ward and Dad's room for the next three days.

Barbara had facial paralysis and lost the use of her left leg and arm. Lucky for them all that her haemorrhage was stopped early on. We stabilised her enough so that she could be escorted home with a medical escort. The family proudly informed us of her progress. During the following months she had extensive physiotherapy to help her to become mobilised. Speech therapy brought her verbal communication almost back to normal. Today I hear she has made an astounding recovery. Barbara told me she would. Her Granddaughters got their Granny back. And an excellent card player she was too.

Although as an interpreter you never imagine that people remember you when they go from our protection. It's very touching when you are thought of after a patient leaves. Grateful patients are so full of good words but quite honestly once they get back on track they seem to forget how indebted they felt. So for us to be recognised and thanked after the event is doubly rewarding.

Heather and Albert went to Australia just twelve months after Albert had a triple By-Pass. Walking through the market lane the other day I heard someone say "That's Gill isn't it?" Albert was such a lovely man, very tall and slim. His heart though was big and fat and somewhat blocked! I remember he came to us, very calm and trying to keep his wife happy. He was alarmed but could do no more than hold himself together. His pain was so intense.

Proved, yet again by another Angiogram, without doubt, he needed a Triple By-pass. The following two days were taken up with frequent calls to the insurance company. They rapidly agreed with what should be done.

Plans for the By-Pass were programmed! And without delay from the insurance company. How extraordinary and unusual but so rewarding. The family gathered around. Two very nice daughters came flying across to help. They settled Mum into a new hotel and took everything calmly and without fuss. Dad with his cheerful, shy smile was very tearful. And very grateful. The day dawned for his big op. We kept a vigil going during the time taken for this massive step. Open heart surgery takes a toll on a families stress level. Invariably they are in constant communication with the rest of their relations.

Albert's recovery went without a hitch in record time. He was flown home. A doctor came for him and he was treated to a first class ticket. Something he will never forget. The day I came across them they whisked me off to their hotel. They all greeted me as an old friend pumping me for information about our little team who had helped so much. How nice to see them again. We get left with untied ribbons when patients leave. When I get to hear of their final recovery my heart closes off the chapter.

Sharon Parker's case was so sad. Not all cases are successful as you can imagine. Thoughts of Sharon remain with me till this day. She was on holiday with her husband. Walking everyday and having a quiet drink and a meal in the evening. Richard had had a scare a few months previously but was now "feeling very fit and well" were his words. The shock was tremendous as one evening he suddenly felt a terrible pain. He had already passed away by the time the ambulance and doctor arrived at the hospital. The next few hours were a blur for Sharon as police and judges came and went. He was taken to the local Chapel of Rest. When things had calmed down a bit we talked. Her insurance company had been informed. And here the shocks waves began! Richard had taken out a new annual policy. He had told Sharon, so she wasn't worried about a thing.

'The amazing policy' which Richard had secured stated that he paid the first £5,000. Obviously that's fine if you go into Intensive Care. The medical bills can be astronomical. The cost of repatriating his body was just £3,900. The local repatriation company arranged everything and Sharon returned with him. I was worried and shocked when she wrote telling me some months later that she had booked for the same week the following year. We were all extremely apprehensive as it didn't seem the normal thing to do. I watched her closely as she had also requested the same room. All she needed to do was to get closure. I understood fully and so made sure I was there for her.

This was one of the sad cases I've dealt with over a decade. Some have been even sadder. My day is never the same and from leaving home you just don't know what will be expected of you next. You have to take it all in your stride and never plan what to say. My experience of life carries me through. I am convinced this is true.

Chapter three
WRONG TIME, WRONG PLACE

If you have a friend who has had an accident whilst away on holiday you will know a bit about the trauma they go through. You may have had the experience too. It may have been simple and stupid. You may have spent months laughing about it! It could, of course have been a disaster! And, on holiday, a lot of common sense should be used. Too often common sense is left behind at the departure airport. Accidents happen unexpectedly, quickly. And,may possibly have been so easily avoided.

91 year old Irene Dean was one of the cases I remember. She fell while out shopping with her daughter. Now looking for a tank top sounds odd for a 91 year old. But surprisingly it was for her granddaughter! "I turned around and lost my leg!" She exclaimed. This caused severe damage to the ligaments in her knee. Resulting in encasement from her groin to her toes in a full plaster cast. We met the next morning when I came on duty. I found her sitting up in bed combing her hair and putting on her best pyjamas! Out came the face creams and make up "Have to look good for my son in law" she proudly informed us. And she did. He was so good to her and they were all a very close family.

Irene was bright and chirpy all of the eight days she was an in patient. But on the day of her discharge we found complications. Her blood pressure was sky high. Not a good indication for a 91 year old, Two days later, with her blood pressure adjusted, we ordered a wheelchair. It arrived for her discharge. But Oh no! it didn't have the leg extension! Now how can a 91yr old lady hold a fully plastered leg in the air? Maintenance hurriedly found a makeshift board and temporarily attached it. She was still smiling though and on reflection thought it great fun.

On her out patient visit a week later she was still sitting on the board but a colourful new sheet was wrapped around it. "Kinder to my bottom" she informed us. And she was still smiling! A fit to fly certificate was readily signed. Her medical escort arrived shortly after, a lovely woman called Helen, to accompany her home. She was just right for our Irene. The family closed up the villa while Irene was off to the airport in an ambulance. They quickly followed in time to see her off as their flight was an hour later. Irene had extra seats of course. She couldn't bend her leg!. It was well worth "the attention I got on my flight, I felt like The Queen" she wrote to tell me. I wonder how long she kept the plaster on. We do know that we had a hand in stabilising her blood pressure and fixing her knee though.

One patient, we'll call her Tracey, froze like a rabbit in headlights, within two hours of arriving on the island. She had been crossing the road, on the zebra crossing. From no where an ambulance, lights on and sirens blaring came racing along the road. It was an emergency and had the right of way. Her friends ran on to the pavement but she froze. There's a message here! In Spain, always look to the left and not the right, when crossing a road! Tracey was lucky as the ambulance braked and just skidded into her. A hair line fracture of her pelvis was the result. No operation was necessary but bed rest for ten days was prescribed.

She patiently waited to be discharged. All the time she was incredibly distressed that her holiday was passing by. Her friends visited regularly although they only stayed for a short visit. They were of course right in saying "We should try to salvage our holidays at least". No holiday for Tracey I'm sorry to say. We know that this was going to be looked into when they got home. She was expecting to get her money back. Tracey was going to hold someone responsible. As the interpreter we are often asked questions about what can be claimed back. It is a subject we can't comment on. Maybe her insurance organised another holiday for her?

Sometimes you are needed and cannot refuse to be on call. When one of our team is summoned out of hours to translate we know it is serious and would never hesitate to respond. You are vital so everything else has to take second place. Not always popular with any of our families or partners unfortunately. Dedication and worth are foremost as you prepare to get into mode.

One evening I was showering. Getting ready to go to my son's parents evening. My phone rang and I had to change plans. Two ladies had been mowed down on the road. From behind! They had been cycling along a well lit area. Also they were correctly on the cycle path. I found them both in A&E, one with a fractured arm and severe grazing and cuts. Sarah was worse off. She had head injuries and a fractured leg and arm. Something struck me as strange though. There were three couples all in suits standing around. One couple came to introduce themselves and very politely told me "we have come straight away, we're from the mission" They were Jehovah's Witnesses. A network is immediately thrown over a situation like this.

All manner of assistance is given with their full and constant support. A couple will be at the bedside day and night. It becomes a little disturbing to find such protection. But everything possible is done for their 'members'. They definitely received legal help too as the man who knocked them down was obviously slightly drunk, not to say legless! They are always there to help their followers. The two ladies recovered from their injuries but will always remember that holiday.

Another potentially devastating case was our ladies from The Isle of Wight. They were embarking on their return flight when disaster struck! The electronic stairs, with a platform to enter the plane, just collapsed! The three ladies were rushed straight to us. As happens with these cases, at first it seems so much worse. Bad enough that this happens at all! But they were relatively 'lucky'. Probably you cannot imagine how. The platform attached to the plane had dislodged and slowly with the weight had tilted. The ladies just slid off and fell to the ground! About four metres drop. Dear Hannah got off with cuts and a sprained arm. Mary and Elizabeth were admitted. Publicity had to be controlled and everything was done for them. Now we all know that accidents do happen but this wasn't their fault. The handlers dealt with it very well and maintained throughout that they were taking full responsibility.

Mary and Elizabeth stayed with us for many days, Mary with a fractured wrist and ankle. She had fallen on top of her friend Elizabeth. Elizabeth needed surgery for her head injuries and she also had a fracture in her spine. They were already best friends on holiday together so were good company for each other. Not easy to keep smiling in these circumstances but they both admitted to us "at least we had our holiday first" They loved all the flowers they got and passed them on to the nurses on leaving. All arrangements were in place for their repatriation. This was carried out by a private company specialising in these cases. They had been contacted and advised of the situation.

The 'repatriation' A stretcher for Elizabeth and a wheelchair for Mary. The doctor and nurse arrived, checked them both and gave final orders to go ahead. Remember publicity was very apparent. Ambulances arrived, along with a PR from the handlers. Filming continued throughout, however disaster nearly struck again as the PR fell down a pot hole near the waiting ambulance. Although certainly not visible in the dark it could have been a double case of potential negligence to be recorded.

Off they went a bit tearful but expressed how happy they were to be "going home at last" Special loading facilities had been laid on as they were not going to go up the stairs normally. Picture them if you can! I was there to encourage them, to help ease their stress and everything went to plan. It was all filmed for the case which would be brought against the handlers. As with these cases we were very happy that they got home alright. The family got in touch to say Mary and Elizabeth were safely in hospital at home.

There are frequent little accidents with people 'falling off pavements' 'tripping up steps' 'slipping on water left by the other clients in the toilets!!!' summer sandals and flip flops are to blame for many of these accidents. 'Twisting their ankle while playing squash' generally some things that could be avoided with common sense. Looking where you are going! But accidents do happen and we will always have patients in hospital while on holiday. They will be annoyed 'Watching the sun go down and their drip go up!'

Sometimes we would give anything to 'put back time' If only they could have done so on this case. We'll call them Patrick and Samantha. They arrived for a secret long weekend. The weather was glorious and after quickly checking into the hotel they made their way to the beach. Nothing was going to stop Samantha going for a ride on the water with the skis. In the north of Majorca we have a very long open beach, perfect for water skiing. That day the wind was up and as they started off in separate boats alongside each other, they had lost themselves in their expectations for the weekend. Not long after doing a turn to come back the other way Patrick, showing off to Samantha, took the wave badly and flipped up!! Samantha took the full force of his skis and yes, you've guessed! Under she went crying out with pain.

Rushed into A&E we promptly diagnosed two fractured legs, severely fractured nose, deep gash on her cheek and side. Not a good state but treatable. Patrick was distraught. Samantha very angry, mixed with severe pain. We patched her up and decided on her treatment plan. Problem here, No insurance. They didn't think they would need it for a weekend BREAK! Well that's what she got, well and truly. He had to think and make plans. No way was Samantha going to let him leave her. Full marks for him, He didn't´.

This story cost him a lot of money. Maybe his marriage too. Take into account the following actions. First, a telephone call to his wife explaining why he wouldn't be back from his ´business course´ on time. Then of course he had so many other arrangements to make including the subsequent urgent phone calls to his bank to arrange a loan!! He had to pay for her repatriation with a Mr Hugo and the private repatriation company. The final cost was around £25,000. Take into account, the unavoidable stretcher repatriation and private ambulance on arrival. Then private hospital and plastic surgery for Samantha´s face. Was it all worth it? That's something we will never know. We cannot keep in touch and get information as to how these patients complete all the treatment they require. Samantha has tried to contact us through a website but we have never followed it up. After all we're not here to judge anyone, we're here to help and listen.

Muriel was another case who arrived almost directly from the airport. Having arrived at the hotel they were walking around the pool to the terrace for their cocktail before dinner. As happens so easily Muriel lost her footing and tumbled into the pool. She hit her hip on the side. You've guessed, she fractured her hip and leg in two places. She couldn't understand how it had happened. She was very confused. And they had no holiday insurance. I explained to her husband James that she could be transferred to an NHS hospital across the island. James refused and decided she should stay with us and be operated immediately. He would be paying for all that was necessary. All this time Muriel was in extreme pain and rambling saying to James" James where are we? I thought we were having a holiday". James answered again and again"Yes Muriel we are but you've had an accident" She continued to be disorientated.

Their hotel was a well known local five star. Maybe she was unable to receive five star accommodation from us. I think she got five star medical treatment though, so did James. We allowed him to stay with her in the room. Poor man he was so very patient with her. A lovely dignified gentleman. Their daughter, Carol, who arrived to help them both, looked just like her father and sounded just like her mother. She also had an exquisite refined English voice. For her own good and with a petition from James and Carol, we slightly sedated Muriel. She was suffering not only from pain but also with her undignified predicament. "I only came for my holiday" She constantly reminded us. As she was elderly, which you may have gathered, she was on numerous medications. Not only did she need all of these but furthermore needed special attention for her various other "beastly ailments".

The situation took a turn for the better when I inquired about any other insurance they may have." Oh Yes "James admitted "I've been paying a private patient's plan for nearly forty years and never claimed anything" "Brilliant" was my answer to that. This could be all sorted. Within two hours they had cover initially for all the medical costs. Things were plain sailing after that apart from having to sooth her feelings over various aspects of her hospital stay. She was ok. Regrettably, but for their own safety, sometimes we have to gently secure patients arms and/or legs. If not we would forever be putting drip lines back in. Worse still could be the resetting of bones after operations. The patient doesn't realise what they are doing hence the slight sedation. But this is always with the families permission. Can you imagine Muriel struggling out of her traction to get to the toilet sorry, "ladies room" "I'm not using that beastly bedpan and you won't make me" was her unvarying reply

They were another example of very pleasant people. I was so glad I was of help to them. Muriel got home safe and sound on a stretcher with a nurse escort all the way. James wrote to me a while later to update me. Muriel's heartfelt thanks and apologise came with it. She was no worse for the experience. Today she is still in a private nursing home near their house. James needed a rest and Muriel remains to a large extent disorientated.

I have dedicated another chapter to general fractures but I must tell you about this case. I'd like to call them Rita and Colin. Colin was devastated and confessed that he felt "such a fool" when he realised that he had let his wife drive across the island. Without knowing she had multiple fractures in her elbow, of course!! The situation was already complicated. They had hired a car in London. Driven across Spain, after arriving on the ferry in Santander. Colin was an excellent navigator at least. But didn't drive. Once in Barcelona another ferry was booked to the island. They enjoyed a busy day in Barcelona, cultural city of Cataluña. But unfortunately, Rita fell up some steps late in the afternoon. The ferry left at 11pm.!She was in pain but however"it was bearable" she told us while being admitted. Colin looking deeply embarrassed at her side.

X-rays showed she had fractured her elbow in at least

three places. Lucky lady didn't lose the use of her arm, as we operated immediately. I had to convince them though as they were due to leave on the ferry the next evening. The reason for their journey to the island had been to visit an elderly aunt. She was 93. Rita saw very little of her and Colin went between the hospital and the Aunt on the local bus. When you work to a tight schedule like they had you never put yourself first. Their plans were rapidly changed. They had to arrange to get a friend to fly out from London to drive them back. An ongoing connection was waiting for them in London! And they had to change that too. Lovely people who were so sensible when faced with a very difficult and inconvenient situation. Don't know what the hire car company said though.

Rita and I had some very interesting chats while she was with us. On her departure a fit to fly certificate and medical report was her proof of her 'accident' for the car hire company. I learnt a lot from them. It is a rewarding and continual experience meeting nice people. But if Rita and Colin ever came this way again I would love to see them both. Wonder if she ever finished her physiotherapy and if it was successful!

Chapter Four
" I´VE GOT AN INSURANCE"

One of the main parts of my job is to liaise with all of the insurance companies. Not an easy or straight forward process. They have a reaction we could call the stalling process. I cannot imagine counting the times an Insurance company has replied " Oh the person who is dealing with this case is on the other line" and / or "has just left her desk. I'll get her to call you back" They very seldom do. I end up calling again on numerous occasions. Now I'm not saying that insurances are hopeless only that sometimes they make our job incredibly more difficult. The insurance is dealing with numbers. We are dealing with people. When holidaymakers are ill they do not need to have all the hassle that an insurance claim involves. In the majority of cases the claim is sorted without delay. I have to deal with all the others. And very distressing it can be. Talk about piggy in the middle.

There are so many cases where the insurance have declined cover. I would like to tell some of these stories. Like to tell you how we resolved the situation. We have never had a patient left on the island to their own device. They have always 'got home'. When a case is declined the wheels are put into action. We have to act quickly and the family rally round. I remember in each of the following stories how the families pulled out all the stops. How Dad "got home just in time for Christmas" How Mum "flew in and was in hospital before the wedding took place" How " Mum was there in a wheelchair, But she was there" It is not only distressing for the families. It is also very costly. Mum may need a medical escort and oxygen on the flight. A stretcher may be necessary. Extra seats may be required. The treating doctor has the last word as he is the one discharging the patient.

Robert was a semi resident. He had been lucky up to now. This time though the medicine given by the pharmacy wasn't enough. His wife Belinda was so worried. Robert was brought into A&E with very severe respiratory problems. A heart attack was on the cards. He'd had warnings before but had taken no notice. His heart wasn't going to last out at the rate it was going. Robert had very acute emphysema. This is a very badly diagnosed condition affecting the tissue in the lungs. Because he wasn't getting enough oxygen around his body his heat was racing. He was on constant oxygen. He was not happy with that. He was on very strong anti biotics through his intravenous drip. Not happy about that either.

The days went by and he didn't seem to be responding. He kept taking his mask off to talk to the man in the next bed. Luckily Arthur was a bit deaf so didn't get the gist of it. He wanted to go out onto the sun terrace. A definite NO that one. The insurance kept in touch but were waiting for the GP check carried out as in all cases. "The GP hasn't given us an answer yet" they told us. He was slowly stabilised but still needed oxygen 24 hours a day. His medication was at a maximum. Unfortunately we received a call from the insurance company declining cover for Robert. He hadn't disclosed the fact that he was using oxygen at home daily. Sometimes a patient decides not to disclose medical facts to their insurance. The reasoning is a mystery. Robert thought his insurance premium would increase considerably. Very silly because his medical bills were far superior to any increase he may have paid.

Belinda came to me desperate to know what to do. "I'll kill him when I get him home" she cried. They owned a flat in the area and so overnight she made some phone calls. The first was Robert's bank. We then gave her a couple of phone numbers of companies who specialise in Medical Repatriations. Roberts's doctor announced that there was no way he could fly without 4 litres of oxygen, per minute, all the way. Now that means he must have a professional person to administer it. It becomes complicated and many times the patient and family think they can just get on a plane. Belinda contacted a company and within a day she had everything in order for his safe transfer to South Wales. A repatriation takes a lot of setting up as flights have to be booked, medical clearance given, admission to hospital at the other end, hotels booked and of course ambulances reserved amongst other things.

The day arrived for Robert's 'repatriation'. He was very nervous but happy to be going home. The medical escort, Mr Hugo, arrived the day before to re assess Robert and talk to the treating doctor. When everything has been approved they give the go ahead. Belinda was waiting for him as he was wheeled down to the ambulance. He still insisted "I can walk you know" Why do these patients think they are making too much fuss. We are only trying to get them onto the flight in maximum condition for flying in these circumstances. All went well for Robert and he got back to Wales and was admitted to his local hospital. He had to continue with his treatment. Belinda was with him all the way. Nevertheless she called me on arrival at the hospital in South Wales to advise me that they were now home.. I have been involved with numerous repatriations both in Mallorca and Tenerife. Some of these stories are from Tenerife.

The following stories are sending the message loud and clear. Get yourself a good insurance and declare everything you can. Most important here is that you have medical screening. This should be in writing. The fault lies in no declaration of previous medical history. Referred to as PMH. All insurance companies will talk to your doctor referred to as a ´ GP check´. Mentioned before this is really a formality. Can you see your doctor telling lies for you? Not likely, the truth comes out.

Olive was a strange case which wasn't covered. She came to us with a fractured wrist. She'd fallen two days previously. Her poor husband was very distressed and so attentive. Having been informed of her medical situation he wanted to take her out and exclaimed he "just intended getting a flight". We strongly advised against that. Her internal bleeding was causing problems. What's more, she needed an operation. Everything was prepared; we were waiting for ´authorisation´ from the insurance company. As alleged before we get stalled by them. However this time they came up trumps. We received it in writing the next day. She was operated immediately and pins put into her wrist. This is normal, especially when the fracture puts the bone out of place. All was going well until one night Olive had a stroke. Not a big one but definitely a stroke.

This is where we started having trouble with her insurance. After numerous phone calls, we determined that she was on medication to help her circulatory situation. Her husband forgot to tell us she was taking aspirin every day. Forgot to tell the insurance too. By this time her daughter was climbing up the wall at home. She got the first flight out to take care of everything. Especially her Dad. He was gradually falling apart. It is very distressing for me too in these cases as we seem so unable to put things right for them.

We transferred Olive over night to the NHS hospital half way across the island. The insurance had sent us an amended guarantee. They stated they would cover all medical costs for her operation but refused to pay for anything to do with her stroke. The whole family were beside themselves. All her medical bills were paid from then on by the NHS. But how was she going to get home?' Again she was put in touch with a repatriation company by the interpreters in the hospital. The NHS will not cover costs for a medical repatriation. When a patient has had a stroke they can be left with slight paralysis. Poor Olive was affected down her left side. Her speech was affected. She couldn't walk unaided and her balance was all over the shop. She was repatriated one night and her daughter telephoned me to tell me the good news. Our nurse, Lets call him Mr Hugo again, came to take her. "He was so nice to my Mum" Her daughter told me when she phoned. It took her many months to recover enough for her to be able to talk better. But she made it.

Another potentially sad case was Joe. He had nearly finished his holiday but was admitted two days before his flight with Pneumonia. His breathing was terrible. Out came the oxygen mask and he was given strong steroids and medication. To open up his airways. The family was in a state as they had to get home for personal reasons. They decided to leave Joe with us. There was no way he could fly anyway. His daughter, Julie, was certain that the insurance company would make sure he got home alright. All went well till the insurance started questioning. Again we realised that Joe hadn't been completely truthful. Not to us or to the insurance company actually. Cover was denied and we informed Joe's daughter. Julie insisted "I don't want Dad to know" Dear Joe was sitting in his suit waiting for the go ahead from the insurance company for his imminent repatriation for days.

In between numerous calls to Julie we managed to get it sorted. But it took the family nearly a week to get everything into place. I had to keep Joe happy with explanations which he could believe. A Mr Hugo arrived with everything necessary for Joe's safe transfer to his home. He also needed oxygen. The repatriation company has their hands tied as they have to go along with whatever the treating doctor advises. Medical clearance is based on the medical report for discharge. Anyway off they went, Joe finally wearing his suit. Mr Hugo was treating him like a king. And Joe loved it. He wasn't too happy when ´Hugo´ made him put the oxygen mask on in the ambulance. But that's what "the doctor ordered" he was informed by his medical escort. So, Joe had to go with the flow. Another case well organised. The whole family were brilliant and had liaised with the repatriation company from the Uk. Had a letter from Julie about a month later to tell me her Dad is now fine but his treatment for his emphysema had been radically altered.

Geoffrey Small was one of those cases when it seems to be just a formality. We expected to receive word of confirmation from the Insurance at any time. It all seemed such a fuss "I feel so much better" Geoffrey insisted. He was on holiday with his wife and their grandson. Having a brilliant holiday until Geoffrey was admitted. His condition seemed to improve. Tests showed a heart attack. He was a model patient, doing what he was told. Geoffrey had had a previous heart attack a few years earlier so knew what was happening. He spent a few days in Intensive Care to be monitored, recovering enough to move to a normal room. I brought his grandson around to below his window in intensive care to see him. He was being sadly missed. As soon as he was stable enough he was moved out to a room. His grandson carried on his card game with Granddad.

Marie was so nice and sensible. She knew Geoffrey couldn't fly until he was declared fit by the doctor. So she agreed that he must stay until then. With everything taken care of she left to take her grandson home to his Mum. We were then very surprised to receive a negative answer from the insurance. To this day we do not know why. I hope they are still fighting the decision. After the statutory time from the heart attack we are able to think about the patient getting home. It is normal to wait for at least ten days. Because of his condition Geoffrey needed a stress test referred to as the treadmill. This was programmed and depending on the result, his return home could be planned.

The day for his stress test arrived. Cardiologist was so sorry to notify him on completion that there was a dangerous level of blockage. He needed a medical escort home. A fit to fly certificate would only be signed by the Cardiologist if this was in place. He was after all responsible for Geoffrey's safe repatriation home. The situation was now very different and distressing for the family. Before leaving the consulting room; Geoffrey had called Marie and told her to set it all up.

Two days later we said goodbye to Geoffrey as he was escorted from the hospital to the airport. Let's call the escort Mr Hugo again. He was flown home with oxygen and medical assistance. He went straight into his local hospital as they were expecting him. And what a lucky man, he was operated on the following week. The blockage was cleared and new stents put in. They both spoke to me shortly afterwards and what a happy couple. Marie's relief knowing her 'time bomb' husband was 'in the clear' was overwhelming. I heard recently that Geoffrey is back at work again.

During the summer months and over the years there has been a certain pattern to declined cases. The majority I suppose are respiratory cases. Possibly undiagnosed or badly diagnosed. These are cases where the treatment has not been sufficient for the patient's condition. Beryl was one of many. She thought, because she had been told, that she had a bacteria living in her lungs. "It has been there for twenty years" She told us her doctor had always maintained. The bacteria turned out to be a very severe level of emphysema combined with long standing asthma.

Beryl spent many days with us, was very breathless but was an extremely good patient.

Our lung specialist, I'd like to call him Lionel, was appalled at the treatment she had been surviving on for so many years. He immediately called for drastic measures, he changed all her medication. Got her on the right road. We were all so pleased until the insurance declined her case. On the grounds of undisclosed medical history we were subsequently informed. The insurance company is well within their right but it is so distressing. Are you getting the message I'm trying to give out?

I pestered the insurance company but they wouldn't change their decision. Now Beryl had a granddaughter who owed her money so dear Beryl was on the phone to her. She was only too pleased to help but suggested that Beryl contact her local MP. A good suggestion as Beryl had once been a local councillor for South Wales. Unfortunately he was unable to help. He explained that the NHS would cover her medical treatment if she moved to an NHS hospital but nothing else. Certainly not a medical repatriation which she needed. Lionel had stabilised her so she was able to fly with oxygen but not without.

Her repatriation was set up with the help of the MP and she left us a few days later. Here comes Mr Hugo again, organising another problem free journey. She was transferred by ambulance in the middle of the night. The medical clearance had to be given for the schedule flight going out of Palma at 05.40. On arrival in London she was taken by ambulance to her local hospital in South Wales. It was less costly and quicker for her this way although it was a long journey. She was comfortable, relaxed and on oxygen all the way. This was one case that never contacted us but we know she was home safely.

There are innumerable cases I could mention but one comes to mind. That is Harvey Budgeon. He was not covered and took it very well. Repatriated by our Mr Hugo. It was at the airport when he admitted that he had piped oxygen at home! "I have to have it for fifteen hours a day. Can't manage without it or I get too breathless" He informed Mr Hugo. "That's the doctors orders". Imagine not declaring that to the insurance. But his doctor did though!!

Our team have all experienced bad advice being given from the GP on many occasions. This was one of the worst and most expensive I think. I remember feeling very angry with Marcia's doctor for his misguided advice. He had suggested she take a flight after 8.00am. The reason for this is as follows. She had piped oxygen at home and was to keep it on all night. She was then going to the airport and taking a two hour flight to Majorca. Oxygen was waiting at the hotel for her in her room. Sounds good organisation so far. But what actually happened was that Marcia arrived in our hospital with very serious respiratory insufficiency. She had done exactly as her doctor advised. Left home after her night's oxygen and had taken the car to the airport. This had taken an hour and a half. She checked in and had to wait for two hours for her flight. The flight was another two hours and then on arriving in Palma had to get the transfer bus to the resort. By the time she had checked into the hotel and got to her room another hour and a half had passed. We are now totalling seven and a half hours. Oxygen doesn't stay in the blood for that time.

Marcia was very ill and of course the insurance declined her case on the grounds of non declaration of medical history. Her doctor may have wanted to save her money on a flight without oxygen but he didn't do her any favours. I think he was very embarrassed when she finally got home. She was repatriated with her husband by our Mr Hugo of course. But there was no advice Hugo could give her about changing the insurance company's decision. Sometimes a doctor's advice is misinterpreted by the patient. Or maybe not interpreted at all.

In most cases of respiratory problems these patients should never have flown anyway. And why didn't the doctor say that? A question I would love to have an answer to but it is almost unbelievable. A very distressing and always costly situation is created which not all families can deal with. The local GP does not have to organise anything. Quite honestly he is not aware of the consequences of his inadequate treatment of these cases- There are more respiratory cases in another chapter but they were all covered by their insurance. A happier and less costly way you can be sure.

Chapter Five
LAW AND ORDER

Without doubt many tourists have found themselves in the following situations. We must make a mention of the police involvement with some of these cases. Many of our patients have had a brush with law and order. It's incredibly easy for merrymaking to get out of hand. Our local police believe all 'holiday makers' are out on the piss. Sorry about the expression. A call is made and plans go into action. It´s not easy for these people to get across to the local police that they are really only having a bit of fun. They don't speak the language. Quite honestly they don't speak any sort of language at that moment. After a night partaking of the local brew it's impossible to make out any sort of decipherable verbal communication.

Big Billy didn't stand a chance as he staggered across the road. A car brushed his side. He was thrown into the air. Landing on the side of his head. He was in a coma on arrival to us. For a couple of days we couldn't even identify him. He had to sleep off the effects. Meanwhile we operated to stitch him up, but the worst was his ´coma´. Two days later, through asking around, his identity was established. Having worked in the same bar for two years he was eventually identified. Unfortunately they refused to have anything to do with him. This is usually the case when police get involved. And the insurance will decline immediately if they get a 'whiff' of alcohol abuse. Mum was contacted and arrived to take him home. How they got home we'll never know as mum signed him out of hospital! I hope he stays in the Uk for a while!!

During the summer we have numerous cases of domestic violence. The police get involved and then they have to take over. More often than not the person who should be pressing charges ends up forgiving his or her partner. It is very sad to see how these people are so frightened and will take it no further. I can understand that not speaking the 'lingo' is a great deciding factor.

I was called out one night to help with translating. A man, Norman, had fallen over the wall at the entrance to his apartment. Some were of the opinion that his wife "must have pushed him" He was brought to A&E accompanied by the police. His wife was duly distressed but seemed more anxious to get home to her daughter. They had been out for the night, visiting their usual haunts. Brenda told us. Arriving back at the apartment around two in the morning, "he couldn't get the key in the door" Brenda reiterated. While Norman was fumbling with the key Brenda decided to take over. She pushed him away from the front door and in doing so he lent against the wall. This is what happened. Norman was a very tall man. His legs were exceptionally long. The wall a regular height. He toppled over into the back terrace of the apartment below. As the police informed us, he landed on his head. A fractured skull was the result. He unfortunately passed away that same night. The police had to investigate.

Brenda returned alone to Birmingham but with a rep from her tour company on the flight with her. Some months later she reappeared for the court case. She was let off for murdering Norman but was declared indirectly responsible, for his untimely death. I wonder if she remembers all we did for her that night. The insurance got Norman home with as little delay as possible under the circumstances. We were informed that she still lives with her daughter and their dogs today.

In my experience some people will go to extreme lengths to save the day after an unexpected turn to their holiday. Recalling one certain case I'd like to call them Darren and Kath. Darren has a time share and his mum Kath was having a holiday with the family. As so easily happens Kath had an accident. She arrived in A&E with a fractured leg and wrist. Typical fall and brittle bones contributing as usual to her condition. The family were in attendance, doing all they could to make her comfortable. "Don't worry Mum we are still making the most of the holiday" They all told her.

She recovered in good time and was ready to go home. The insurance was sending Mr Hugo. The day came and Hugo was to re assess Kath for travel. Darren was fussing around and very concerned with Mum's luggage. He was assured that all would be taken care of by Hugo. Darren and the family would be leaving two days later.

The ambulance arrived and Darren too with Mum's personal belongings. He repeatedly asked Hugo to make sure ".she doesn't lose her luggage. As we aren't with her will she remember to pick it up?" Off they went to the airport for their flight to Manchester. On arrival all Hugo had left to do was make sure that the wheelchair was taken past the luggage belt for Kath's luggage. He has done this so many times but was to report to Darren when they were safely in the ambulance on way to the local hospital. He was quickly pulled aside by the customs men. "Sir, Is this your luggage?" demanded the seriously looking custom men. "Actually no it isn't "was Hugo's hurried answer.

On inspection, as demanded, Hugo and Kath discovered that all her personal belongings were really 56 sleeves of cigarettes. "You are not allowed that many" was the information given by these serious men. Kath was horrified and very embarrassed. Hugo, I must admit, was slightly cross, to say the least. Kath's luggage was confiscated of course. Darren admitted that he was only trying to recuperate some time and expenses lost for his Mum. "I'll be bringing her belongings back with me". He informed Hugo as they arrived at the local hospital. Luckily she didn't need her smalls. I think he was hoping to make a lot of money too. The customs men were only doing their job after all. They are the law and order. Message here is accept the circumstances when "The sun goes down and the drip goes up".

It is quite embarrassing for the family when a patient is escorted by the police on arrival at hospital. One young girl called Sadie was brought in at two in the morning. She had had the top section of her finger bitten right off. Sadie and her sister were at the local club dancing away. The story goes that it was Sadie's turn to get up onto the pedestal to give her exhibition. The girl already there didn't agree. Sadie tried to claim her "spot". The other girl opposed this. A fight broke out. In the scuffle Sadie got in a head lock. Natural reaction was to retaliate.

She pulled the girls hair. During the fight, which by now had a lot more people joining in, Sadie's finger was bitten unmercifully. The unnatural strength of the girl and her bite actually bit all the way through the joint. Here we have a situation of grievous bodily harm. The police were on the scene in no time and the culprits were all arrested.

After treatment at the hospital including an operation Sadie was accompanied by her Mum to make an official complaint. Mum, Dad and sister were all there trying to avoid contact with the offender. The police were adamant that charges should be brought as this was serious. Finally it all became clear that the wrong doer had been on drugs but she was still very guilty. The court case came up a few months later and justice was done. However nothing could make up for the loss of the top joint of Sadie's finger. She will have to recall the incident all her life. Again the police were astounded at the behaviour of the tourist.

Unquestionably during the busy summer months we see a baffling number of cases where the police will be involved. Very strong shots and shorts could possibly be to blame. Angus was rolling when admitted and the police who accompanied him adamant that he should have a breath test performed. They wanted proof that he was indeed very drunk. While the police were talking to the doctors he escaped out of the back entrance. He was chased and brought back in. Tests were pending and a drip put up. Angus couldn't catch on why his bag had been confiscated.

Angus's belongings contained two half bottles of vodka and a bottle of gin with a cheap carton of wine at the bottom. It was discovered that he was alone on holiday.

When we finally deciphered his personal circumstances it became clear that he was trying to forget about a recent divorce. The police cannot ignore this but quite honestly are not interested. The main concern to them is that this man was creating havoc all due to drink. Our patient continued to escape whenever it became possible but was brought back each time. Finally he sobered up sufficiently to take his coach from the hotel to the airport. His tour operator was not happy but ecstatic that their problem customer was on his way home.

The local police cannot deal with the cases fairly. They consider these tourists are breaking the law. "Wouldn't be allowed to get away with this behaviour in their own country" is their reasoning. While I agree with this it is necessary for us to pick up the pieces and help to rescue the situation in time. Occasionally the patient will sleep off the effects and charges are dropped if the outcome is not too serious. Once again a question of saving the day. The well earned holiday will be saved too

Chapter six

"GRANDAD'S ON HOLIDAY"

During the holiday months and especially in the winter period we see a lot of elderly people holidaying alone. It's a pleasure to see these people enjoying themselves. They join in all the activities organised for them. Take a stroll along the front. Watch ´Only fools and horses´ in the local bars perhaps for the fiftieth time.´ ´Have tea and biscuits in the afternoon´ ´play bingo" to name but a few. Generally relax and enjoy milder weather than they would have in the UK. Sometimes the families have ulterior motives and the elderly relative is packed off to give the rest of the family a respite. This isn't always the case but I remember a lot of times when this is so.

Richard was on holiday with a friend. Now his family didn't know his friend but were happy he was going for a nice break in the sunshine. Richard hadn't mentioned he was travelling with his "friend" a lady!. Richards wife was furious when she discovered the situation and refused to help in any way. They were two days into the holiday when Richard fell in the rain. Yes! he fractured his hip. He was alone on arrival. And stayed that way throughout his hospital stay. The friend, we'll call her Thelma, didn't show up. She was on her holiday! He had no clothes, in fact he had nothing at all.It remained that way for most of his stay. Many times I had to tell him to close the back of his hospital gown. Not very pleasant for the people behind him. And embarrassing for Richard too. Now Richard was a bad tempered old soul, He was very difficult to handle and as the days passed became more so. None of his personal belongings arrived. We had only his insurance. That was good planning on Thelma's part anyway.

The reception staff were by now avoiding calls from room 319. They were very busy and Richard was being very demanding, and very rude. Poor man couldn't understand why Thelma wasn't answering his telephone calls. I could! I called the Rep and explained what was happening and what we needed. She told us what we already knew "Thelma is on holiday" I had asked for all his things to be sent over from the East Coast. But who was to pay? Not Richard by the looks of things. Finally this was resolved. The patient's suitcase arrived via the airport and a local hotel. But on the other hand still no Thelma. His holiday was over the next day. I understand Thelma flew home on the original flight. I was in touch with Richard's wife. She wasn't too helpful either. I gave up!

Richard recovered enough so we could get him home. He had physio sessions so we could get him mobile. We had to move numerous patients out of his room. It appears he was demanding help from them too. Dear man only wanted a bit of attention. The insurance company finally repatriated him with a nurse, not Hugo, and wheelchair assistance. Off he went with his suitcase, clutching his passport in his hand. I was glad to know he was at last going home. Hope he was as well looked after as he had been with us.

Deirdre, not her real name, of course, always holidayed in January, alone. She would arrive at the airport, in a wheelchair, and all her medical necessities. She had serious problems with diabetes and epilepsy. On arrival she would demand assistance to the coach from the reps. Well she couldn't manage her wheelchair, push her case and" all my medical things too, can I?" she would reason with the reps. Always choosing the same hotel, but was never there very long. Each year she would be found the following day in the toilets of the hotel. " I don't remember a thing" She mumbled as a doctor was called who admitted her to the hospital.

In the hospital she received all the medical attention necessary. But this happened every year until she was black listed by the tour operator who by then had rumbled her game. Once admitted she became very demanding with the nurses who were far too busy to attend to her every whim! I was too but always treated her with respect and normal attention as with every patient. There was really nothing wrong with Deirdre, except for the fact that her medication needed to be taken regularly and as prescribed. Whether this was done 'deliberately' I will never know for sure. After a few days she would be discharged to the hotel. Some years she would be readmitted days later! All she needed was some TLC which she wasn't getting at home or from her family. When she was blacklisted by a well known tour operator she switched to another. And she ended up in our hospital just the same the following year.

Not all elderly people are 'fit to fly' But they still arrive for their holiday. Not always booked personally by themselves. Perhaps it was a welcome gift not usually received from relatives. The seriously chronic cases are the saddest. They are admitted to the hospital within a short time. It's no joy for them and they are generally very lonely patients. I always consider that it could have been my Mum or Dad in that bed. And treat them accordingly. The worst time is when they get refused cover by the insurance company. I've covered that in another chapter. I know these patients can be very difficult to deal with but honestly I don't know what the answer is. It would be so much kinder if there were more special centres available in the Uk where families could send their relatives to give them a little rest!. Maybe there are? What I am sure of is that the majority of these cases should never have flown.

The general condition of the elderly makes it so easy for them to have an accident and the main problem I have when they are admitted, is to obtain their medication. Invariably the answer we get is "It's in my room at the hotel, on the table by the bed" One thing the local doctors and I find very confusing is British patients carry little boxes with their pills set out with daily supplies labelled for specific days. The treating doctor asks the patient "what is this tablet, what is it for?" They don't know! So another message here, 'take your prescription with you if you have numerous medications'. In Spain medications are administered in individual boxes with the contents and name listed. Much easier for me, and the doctors too, at a glance.

I feel we all go through the same thought process. Do we accept the fact that we are not getting any younger and can't do what we could? Andrew was one of many. He continued his daily swim. One such day he was pulled onto the beach in a semi conscious state by the lifeguard. The ambulance arrived and the doctor managed to get him to A&E. "I just felt myself being sucked onto the rocks" he muttered. All day he insisted, in his befuddled state "I'm normally a very good swimmer". He was lucky to have been seen in time.

Andrew was 85 and was not very stable on his pins to say the least. He had been holidaying alone for years, "with the family's permission" Yes, I'm sure about that. He was on warfarin, so due to his fall on the rocks, had serious internal bleeding. This resulted in numerous black bruises all over his body. The family was contacted but although they remained in contact with us no one came to support him. "We are all working you see" was the reply. Of course we did our best for him and made sure that suitable patients went into the accompanying bed. He was never alone and made some good friends. He was lovely and told me some cracking jokes. Wish I had written them down.

The time came for him to leave us and get home. Hugo arrived and cheered him up. "Don't you think it's time to give up swimming in the sea?" He inquired. Andrew's reply was well thought out. " I've been swimming since I was six. Why should I give up while I'm still enjoying it?" Hugo was lost for words but replied "Maybe someone is trying to tell you something"

Andrew went home quite happy. We are usually updated on these cases even if only by the insurance company. This time it was Hugo who told us. Hugo used a company that specialised in road transfers of patients on arrival in the Uk. Rod was his real name. He was waiting at the airport for them both, taking as usual great pride in his appearance as he did with his vehicle. His ´ambulance car´ was a luxury Mercedes complete with medical equipment including a stretcher. The stretcher could be converted into luxury seating when required. He always wore a suit and was extremely nice to everyone. He was well known and liked by all.

This particular day Andrew was very chatty and persuasive. He needed some bits and pieces from the supermarket so Rod agreed to detour. Unfortunately the story takes a bizarre turn here. Rounding a street corner they came upon a police road block. A man brandishing a gun had held up the supermarket. Andrew was all for getting out of the car and going to have a closer look. He hadn't reckoned on Rod though. Rod's professionalism saved the day again, He was after all taking a repatriated patient home. .Andrew didn't get his shopping and was delayed by the police for a further hour. He chewed Rod's ear off though. Probably to this day Andrew is still swimming whenever he can.

You will have noticed that I spoke of Rod in the past tense. As a special tribute to him I wanted to mention his good work. He was seriously missed by Hugo and everyone who worked with or for him when he died, a couple of years ago, after a relatively short illness. Always professional and a real gentleman. he was maybe one of very few left. He was a retired fireman and took his ´new business´ very sincerely. Thanks for all the repatriations Rod, though I never had the pleasure of meeting you I did feel I knew you.

There are many cases I could mention in this chapter

but they are too numerous. So I'll save them for my next book. When another such case is admitted we do our best for them as we do with everyone else. It can just be so sad to see how lonely these people feel and how they blossom out with the attention they are getting. At the end of the day they all deserve their holiday, don't they?.

Chapter Seven
AN UNWELCOME BREAK

While on holiday some people will remember their dreamed of two weeks break as being their unwelcome 'break'. Finding themselves in situations, possibly unavoidable. Families are kept sitting around a waiting room for their relative to be diagnosed. Not to be recommended. Here are some stories of fractures. "We're off on our well deserved break" exclaimed the excited queuing masses for their departing flight. They couldn't imagine how easy and too often accidents can occur.

Around the time of the Olympics, very enthusiastically, Martin tried to copy an Olympic dive. He did a 360º roll. And cut his head on the side of the pool. " Watch me Dad" He shouted over. Straight into hospital he came and had eight stitches inserted. Donald was competing in a "Gladiator's Knock out" on the bouncy castle. To impress the kids! He landed awkwardly on his leg and his tibia fractured from his ankle upwards to his knee. And he was winning at the time! His son wasn't impressed, even more so when he had to push him around in a wheelchair for the rest of the holiday.

Barry could have lost his arm. He had taken off his

gold chain before going down the 'kamikaze' in the water park. But he had forgotten his watch! He came to us, sirens blaring, with a severed artery above his wrist. The bleeding was stopped with difficulty and suturing was complicated. He had to have the sutures removed as the bleeding started again and was re-sutured inside. I do believe his scar will be barely visible in time. It was so well done by the Traumatologist on call that day. It could have been considerably worse. Think about it.

Paul arrived at the hospital with both ankles fractured! He'd fallen off the stage at the disco! "It was higher than we thought" He told us. Being almost legless and having fallen he then proceeded to crawl out of the club. After a short sleep induced by his 'wee drink', he woke to excruciating pain. Luckily a passer by called an ambulance. It was then 8.15 am. When I enquired why no one was alarmed as he was crawling out, his reply was "everyone else was crawling out too". His friends spent just a few hours laughing at him. By then they had considerably sobered up.

Anji spent the most part of a month here after her son had his accident!!. We became friends. Although I could do nothing to ease her situation, I was there for her. Sean had tripped while coming down the steps of 'the club'. He had consequently toppled into the fountain, hitting his head and fracturing a vertebrae. On holiday with a group of friends, he had been persuaded to "stay out on the circuit and put away a few more shots". A huge mistake it turned out to be! Injuries sustained during accidents like this are rarely reversible. Sean's were not. He still remains today, paralysed from the chest down.

His Mum, Anji, had not been happy about this

holiday from the moment all the boys from the football club starting talking about it. We talked at length about life and coping with what is 'our lot'. Her fears had not been unfounded. And the worse happened. Today Sean is in a wheelchair but living in a flat, purpose built for his needs. All of his friends have raised money constantly to help his future. They feel so responsible for what happened. Sean, dear lovely blue eyed Sean. His future plans involve learning to operate a computer. First he must have an operation to graft some ligaments from his legs to his fingers. From the sixth vertebrae down he has lost any control of his fingers, He can still move his hands and shoulders though .I know he is still smiling and has not lost that direct look he had with those intriguing blue eyes. " Tell me the truth please, will I ever walk again?" was the question he asked me relentlessly. We exchange emails now and again. He has accepted 'his lot' and knows he will never walk again! But, wishes he hadn't been in the wrong place at the wrong time

One of the most dangerous times is when it's raining. Young and old are all potential sufferers. What a shock one rainy day. We had five patients admitted with fractured hips. Not young. Not old. But all ages. We doubled them up as we could. Not too kind to the nurses though. Extra work is involved with these patients. Because they are bedridden and helpless. Poor Edith thought she wasn't getting as much attention as Rose. It was both their left hips!!!. Rose was mobile and out of bed before Edith. My goodness but Edith did try. They were turned at the same time. Bed bathed at the same time . If one had "bed sores coming" so did the other. If one wanted a bedpan. So did the other. The families got as bad. Whatever medication

Rose was given. "Why isn't Edith taking the same" was the husband and daughter's question.

The day for repatriation arrived and what a fuss. Rose was returning with a nurse escort and a wheelchair. All arranged and agreed on. Happy as Larry till Edith got her information. The families were not happy when I went to visit. Edith was also going with a nurse escort. But, "how come she is going on a stretcher! "angrily inquired her daughter.. Now Edith was a bigger lady and couldn't have struggled in and out of wheelchairs all day. Insurance companies will take everything into consideration when setting up a ´medical repatriation´. Each patient has different needs and has to get home with the least of fuss and pain. Thank goodness they weren't discharged the same day. At least they didn't have to travel on the same flight!!!

Most unfortunate was a fracture on a fracture. Sounds odd I know. Denise had fallen in the hotel. She was already wearing a strong elastic bandage. But this was to safeguard a recent fracture. Her husband fussed around her. She was loving it, hubby not so much. He was on holiday, wasn't he? All day he was on and off his laptop. "Doing business "He insisted. Quite upset when I told him we didn't have free WiFi to connect up to! "This is a hospital" I reminded him several times.

He found a corner and used his router, I think! We could all hear his deals going on though. He spoke a bit of Spanish so was chatting up the nurses too. Poor Denise was fitted in between his business deals. She left us nearly as good as new. Went back to square one as far as physiotherapy was concerned though. She wouldn't be able to walk for a further six weeks on that leg. He did see her safely home at last. With extra seats of course. He had to pull out all his business skills when the insurance company were dragging their heels. His laptop was working overtime.

It is very upsetting when we cannot put things right for a patient. Debbie had fallen while on her way back to the hotel. She shouldn't have taken the short cut. But there you are, she did. A very nasty fracture of her femur was the result. It should have been operated that night but as with all cases we have to wait for authorisation from the insurance. My first few hours on duty were spent phoning the insurance assistance company. My goodness were they slow? Everything was prepared. The operating theatre was on call for her. I was so sorry for Debbie when the insurance came back with the idea that they would repatriate her instead of letting us operate. She was in considerable pain and spent all day crying..

There was nothing I could do even though Debbie, and her family were hopping well not exactly, mad! A nurse arrived two days later to take Debbie home. She had a special wheelchair for her. Didn't satisfy her though. She had special boarding facilities. That didn't make her happy either. I think by the time she got home Debbie would have thawed out a bit though. I did hear she went on a waiting list at her local hospital. That would have been the last straw for Debbie. She could have had it all done with us and case closed.

Clive, not his real name of course, fell in the hotel while on holiday with two lady friends. He was admitted in excruciating pain and shouted at me because they had to move him from the stretcher to the bed. He became slightly more good-natured as the days went by but my goodness was he bad tempered. On falling he had fractured his hip. It was a hairline fracture only but still a fracture. His pain was well controlled even though he made such a fuss. The other problem I had with Clive was his asthma. He had to be on oxygen all the time. He had his own sprays which were not enough due to the shock he suffered. The doctor instructed him to remain on complete bed rest because of the pain. When the insurance company started asking questions about his respiratory situation he blamed me for opening my mouth. We have to tell the truth in all cases. Sometimes we can bend things but tell lies, No.

At one time while waiting for the GP check the insurance phoned Clive and did mention he may not be covered. Of course he was angry and was waiting for me when I arrived. His temper flared and he accused me again of "telling the insurance things. If they don't cover me it's your fault" He shouted. When he'd calmed down I explained how they worked. After that he progressed to being a bit more agreeable but not a lot. Clive spent quite a few days with us meanwhile his lady friends returned home. His pain subsided somewhat with strong painkillers and at last the insurance covered his case. Finally they got him home in a wheelchair with a nurse to help him. No it wasn't "Hugo" again.

During these past ten years of course I have seen many cases where people have fallen badly. Elsa was one case which could have had fatal consequences. She had fallen off a chair on her balcony. This doesn't sound serious enough to be fatal but she fell very awkwardly and on her head. She was in a coma when she arrived at the hospital. A brain scan showed slight bleeding in the area. We kept her under observation and after a couple of days her condition was much improved. After the first alarm I was pleased to inform her family that all was well. The bleeding had not worsened and she was back at the hotel before the end of the holiday time. She flew back on her original flight. I never heard anymore from them so all must be well.

All the cases in this chapter could have had very different outcomes and as you can figure out it is so easy for accidents to happen while on holiday. There are so many more but I'll save them for the next book.

Chapter eight
"I DIDN'T THINK IT WAS THAT SERIOUS"

When planning a holiday the majority of our patients have seen their local doctor before travelling. They may have asked for medication to last for their time away. Asked the doctors advice about flying. Very rarely do they ask for a letter saying they need a buggy or wheelchair assistance. There is a potential problem here. The doctor will inevitably say "the holiday will do you good! you go away and enjoy yourself" Does he ever put that in writing? The answer is No. A flight for most people will take a toll on their body. If a person is not in good health it will cause considerable changes.

Some of the holiday makers who are admitted do not realise how serious their condition is. They may have never been diagnosed at all. A frequent question I have to translate is "so why are you taking this medication?" Not many know or cannot imagine that they are as serious as they really are. I don't think patients are in the habit of asking detailed questions to their GP. Conditions are not discussed in depth. One patients GP actually admitted to the Insurance assessor that he hadn't told his patient that he was suffering from acute angina attacks. Therefore the patient honestly didn't know. How could he have declared his previous medical condition? The following cases are typical of these situations. Some have a happy ending, some don't.

Our Mr Hugo related this case to me when we were discussing some insurance problems. Going to her GP to ask advice seemed to be sufficient for Annette. She was planning on visiting her daughter in South Africa for three weeks. He provided her with all her jabs and medication to last for her time away. All well prepared and thought out. Well that's what she thought.

On arrival in South Africa and her daughter's beautiful home she was taken, within hours, to the hospital. No one, at least her doctor, hadn't given a moments thought to the fact that her holiday destination was some 4000 metres above sea level. Not recommended when you have a fairly severe respiratory condition. The air was so thin pf oxygen she couldn't breath and spent her three weeks in a hospital bed. Taken home eventually by Hugo. Doctors are unaware it seems of the changes in the body while flying. Maybe there should be a section relating to aero medicine in a medical students studies.

This case is not only true but also the names are too. I have been given permission to use them by the patients wife. It's one of those times when I have remained friends with the family. Tony and Irene Prescott were going on holiday with their daughter and her family. Something they did every year. Tony had been a bit low for a few weeks previously but put it down to tiredness. He had been a diabetic for years. Irene was worried about him but carried on with preparations for their departure. Too many people would have been disappointed. Paul, their son in law had been saving all year. Everything was packed except last minute items to be put in the case , tickets, passports and insurance. Irene, being extremely organised had tabs on everything.

Irene rechecked her insurance and then she was worried. Not having read the small print before. And how many people do? The small print gets smaller every year. It stated that if one question had been answered with "yes" then the person was not covered unless medically screened previously. Now Irene is a very practical person. She started ringing around and eventually got cover for them both. With minutes to spare, for they were about to close, she got the go ahead from the insurance doctor. She had no papers but a reference number. What a godsend that turned out to be.

The family arrived at their hotel where Tony immediately laid down on his bed and told Irene "I think you'd better call a doctor, I really don't feel well" He came to us in record time and was admitted straight into intensive care. All tests were carried out in a very short time and showed his kidneys were failing, had been for a while. His diabetes was completely uncontrolled. It was touch and go for many days. All the family gathered around but could do nothing only be together. A dialysis machine was brought in. He was on constant monitoring and oxygen. However the doctor promised throughout that he would stabilise Tony enough and would get him home. This was what Irene held onto. She was so positive he would.

Now, the worst part for the family was when the

holiday was nearing the end. The week was up. Joanne, their daughter, Paul and the kids had to leave. The tears shed were so emotional. Tony has a sister who lives in Alicante. She flew across to take over. Irene was booked into a hotel opposite the hospital by the insurance. Anne joined her. The hotel ,let's call it our hospital hotel, is very caring and knew of Irene's case. We tend to always use this hotel if possible because everyone who is in the same situation gravitates together. "You just know when someone walks up the path that they have someone in hospital" I've been told many times.

After two aborted attempts, an air ambulance was on its way. Tony was going home. He had been stable for 24 hours. The doctor was satisfied that he would make the journey so gave the go ahead to the insurance doctors .Twice having been cancelled it was with caution that the air ambulance crew arrived. When the doctors on the flight saw Tony they had to reassess him. His medical notes had been sent over and they were expecting the worse. He was finally declared stable enough to leave as planned. It took two hours to prepare him for the flight but off they went. Irene thought it amusing she was asked to go to the toilet before leaving the hospital. She understood when she set eyes on the plane. There was no toilet of course as the plane was a small air ambulance. She was glad she did what they told her.

The ending of this story is sad because Tony died a little more than three months after returning to Manchester Hospital and finally his home town of Wigan. During that time, he only got home for a couple of visits. His family still keeps his memory constantly alive today. Their experience may help others to realise how important a suitable insurance is. This is the message in this book. Irene, as many others, is so grateful for the attention she received. While Tony was in hospital everyone from start to finish did their best. Insurance companies do pull out all the stops. Their support is invaluable. So too is the unexpected support from strangers and onlookers. People in the hotels and other patients families. Irene wanted them all to know how she could never, never repay them. We are still friends today.

A case of misdiagnosis brought this patient to us. I'll call her Ingrid. She arrived with her family and was enjoying a few days in the sun. Her severe headaches continued until she finally had to call a doctor. She was whisked into hospital. And after initial tests she had a brain scan. A large shadow showed up behind her eye. We immediately thought she had a brain tumour. Further investigations allowed us to diagnose an abscess behind her eye. By the time we had cleaned and syringed her sinuses she was in a bad way. Her son and husband informed us that she had been having bad headaches for six weeks treated by her GP as 'migraine'. We did what we could but there was a danger of general sepsis. An infection which goes around the body through the blood and eventually affects the vital organs. This can be fatal of course. She was close to sinking into a coma.

I remember we fought with the insurance company for an air ambulance. At first they wanted the family to contribute half. Full marks to the insurance as they finally agreed to organise one. Ingrid was taken home with her son and husband. We heard she died six weeks later with all her family at her side. The insurance company called to say that our arguments and perseverance for an air ambulance had swayed their decision. They knew, as we did, she was not going to pull through. But she was home.

As a comforter and hand holder as goes with our work we try our very best in difficult situations that can arise. Our team enjoys celebrating when we feel we have achieved the outcome that a patient deserves. We would love to be able to do this with every patient we deal with in distressing situations.

Alan was a bad case of cellulites in his leg. He was a big man, took up most of the bed. He spent days with his leg elevated on the bottom part of the bed. He would have loved to take that bed home with him. He had the deepest blue eyes I have ever seen. His smile was contagious and he kept every one of the patients who ended up in the other bed happy and laughing. He told me a joke which I still laugh at. Alan was actually very ill so I want this joke to go in here.

A man went to look for a job at the local blacksmiths. "Have you ever shoed a horse "asked the man in charge. "No" replied the man" But I've told a donkey to f… off ". I laughed for months at that one.

The patient admitted in the next bed was feeling better in minutes. He was discharged soon after. Alan remained with us and seemed to be getting worse. As he was a long term diabetic we could not get his medication to remain at an acceptable level. Every two hours a poultice was placed on his leg with special water and medication applied. Still on a drip feed with very strong and supposedly effective anti-biotics. He did everything the doctor said but he wasn't responding as he should.

We sent him down to our sister hospital for a

special deep tissue X-ray. Returning the same day he then proceeded to have a heart attack during the night. Rushed back down we did an emergency 'Angiogram' He was lucky as two stents did the trick. For his cardiac condition anyway. We still had to sort out his leg. Finally he was able to get out of bed and the cellulites improved. His medication was regulated and he is much better today. He's lost a bit of weight too, not a bad thing. His lovely wife was happy.

Over the next few days he became more stable and then the insurance were instructed to start looking into a repatriation plan for him. His brother and his wife had remained on the island to support Alan's wife which they did very well. Now he would be going home as soon as the statutory time was up. Remember when a patient has had a heart attack they mustn't fly for at least ten days. Ten days were up and the family saw Alan being prepared for his imminent departure. His medical escort, you are right! Mr Hugo had arrived. He was sorry to be going. We were glad to see the back of him, though for the right reasons. At one time I thought he would never leave in a normal way. Another person whose life we helped to save, thank goodness.

Gall stones exist! Gall stones are hidden away until they cause trouble. One lovely lady, we'll call her Carol, was on holiday with her partner and their two young daughters. She was seen by the hotel doctor when she awoke one night with terrible abdominal pain. Brought into A&E she was admitted for observation and diagnosis. An ultrasound showed up gallstones. During the next few days she was on strong anti inflammatories and anti biotics. Her partner took the children home. He returned the following day. The stone remained lodged in the bile duct not moving one way or another. With authorisation from her insurance company we sent her to our sister hospital for a special test. A camera is put down through her stomach and takes a photo of the 'stone'. At the same time little tweezers are used to remove the stone, if possible.

Carol came back to us with the stone removed. I was so pleased for her and she was in high spirits and very cheerful. I always went to see her before I left for the day for a little chat as she was missing her children so much. That day she was a bit down but I got her to smile before I went. Coming on duty the next day I was disappointed to be told she was in Intensive Care again. During the night she had started haemorrhaging which can happen sometimes with this kind of operation. Poor girl was beside herself, she had been so looking forward to getting home as soon as possible. John, her partner was comforting her but she was heartbroken. There was nothing we could do but control the haemorrhaging and wait.

It was only a few days later, but it seemed an eternity for Carol, the insurance sent out a doctor to take her home with John. She had a photo of her children constantly by her bed which got mislaid the last day. The photo turned up a few months later in ICU, it had slipped between some papers. I was relived to send it on to her. Carol lost a lot of weight during her hospital stay. Although she was really pleased about this she could have chosen a more sensible way of dieting.

As I have said from the start of this chapter many conditions are undiagnosed or badly diagnosed before we even examine the patient. One lady. Marion, who I recall so well was dumbstruck when she was diagnosed with diverticulitis by our specialist. This is when the intestine gets blocked and twisted because of infection basically. Having been complaining for such a long time she couldn't believe that nothing had been determined by her GP. Admittedly, I know through personal experience, the doctors will look for a simpler diagnosis first. She was initially treated for gastroenteritis but as she was not responding to the treatment we investigated further. Through an ultrasound and tests it was proved that the obstruction and diverticulitis was now in a critical condition. The medication she received helped to unblock the area. She had to go on to very strict treatment with nil by mouth for days.

Her husband eventually moved into the hospital with her. I discovered by mistake, because Marion hadn't wanted to tell us, that her husband had dementia. She had to write everything down for him even what he should eat and at what time. They were both so much happier and Marion very reassured when we did this. She recovered sufficiently to start eating again but it took quite a few days.

Eventually she was ready to go home. We spoke to the insurance company who started planning. It normally takes only a few days to organise but they are dealing with many cases. When waiting and in the summer it seems too long for an individual who is desperate to return to normality and to get back to work. She went off very happy with a complete and up to date medical report for her GP.

All my colleagues will agree with me when I say that

so many if not all the patients remain in our minds for a long time. Having supported these people through some very nasty experiences we can't disconnect easily. They could all tell their stories too.

I cannot go into a certain hospital in Majorca without thinking of the next case. A few years ago now but remembering the patient I'll call Malcolm. He was admitted with pancreatitis. A severe inflammation and infection of the pancreas. He was so very seriously ill when he got to us. Admitted immediately into intensive care he was put onto life support. Remaining under sedation for many days it was weeks before he was able to go home. Malcolm's wife stayed with him on the island until his safe return home. At one stage he was so ill that Pat, his wife, stayed in the hospital all night fearing the worse.

He had many setbacks during his treatment but in the end was recovering well. The family decided to travel to the island to see him and were always popping in when he was moved to the ward. The ward here in Spanish hospitals are normally two or three beds to a room.

Malcolm's pancreas was not in a good condition from years of abuse. By that I mean through his diet as well as his habit of a little tipple. He learnt to re educate his palette and enjoyed some foods which he would never have tried had he not spent so long with us. I hope even today Malcolm, if you read this book and recognise your case, that you are as healthy as the day you left us. I have a lovely photo of Malcolm and Pat the day they were repatriated after seven weeks here. It is in a draw and came to light when I was looking for some papers.

I am so glad that I was involved with these cases and wish them all good health and if they remember us here I hope they are behaving, medically that is. And enjoying a full life. These are just some of the cases I recall but could mention so many more too. They were no less important to us and the outcome good. I'd like to remember them all. Maybe your story will appear in my next book, let's wait and see.

Chapter nine
NO BREATHING PROBLEMS

One winter I was lent to Tenerife to continue my work as an interpreter. During the five months there problems and situations were the same. The amount of respiratory cases is always very prominent. The "Calima" and "Sciroco" are typical winds found in the seven micro climates present in the Canary Islands. They do, of course, cause respiratory changes in people with respiratory problems. In Majorca we also get different winds and the humidity causes havoc with these patients. Many patients develop conditions they never knew they had. And invariably end up in our hospital beds.

My first case to interpret was Molly she was rather poorly with severe respiratory insufficiency. Going to her room on the first day her condition was causing some concern. My thoughts were" she should really be in intensive care" Not being the doctor it's not easy to give an opinion. The family were so concerned. But the next day on returning to see her I was astonished to discover she was in intensive care. It was as though the doctors had heard my thoughts. Later on comments were made regarding this to the family. She was treated accordingly but took a turn for the worse.

Molly remained in intensive care for quite a while. She had to be intubated which is when a patient needs to be put on assisted breathing. A tube is inserted through their airways into their lungs. This allows the patient to recuperate and the doctors to improve the respiratory condition. The patient is sedated and is not aware of the seriousness of their circumstance. Molly's husband George remained by her side all the time but meanwhile the rest of the family took turns to return to the Uk. The best of treatment brought her back to a sufficiently stable condition to be ready for home. Her daughters and son were delighted that they would at last have her with them again.   George and Molly returned with a 'Mr Hugo' to a grand celebration party. Slowly, she regained her original dress size. During her hospital stay Molly lost a great deal of weight so that George had to buy all new clothes for her repatriation. Even her bra was too big. Molly was a lovely patient and remains in my mind till today. When they are around for so long it is understandable they grow to be firm friends.

Joanie was a most extraordinary case. We were soon to find out that she weighed in the region of thirty five stone. She became ill in the apartment. Her husband not knowing what to do. A weeks run around on her motorised scooter was all the holiday she had. Being in a third floor apartment it was extremely difficult for her to be moved. The ambulance men, called by the doctor, had to get her down stairs to place her out into the ambulance. She was in a grave state of respiratory insufficiency. Risk of a cardiac crisis were evident. Oxygen and emergency medical attention was needed without delay. Portable equipment was put into place while a decision was made as to how 'to transport' this rather large patient.

The local fire brigade was summoned. No sirens though! As it was impossible for a stretcher to be used in the lift the firemen used their long ladder to reach the apartment balcony. Joanie's husband, Oscar, looked on as she was placed into a cradle used to remove injured people from fires. At one point Fabian, the ambulance man, almost collapsed and was close to being crushed between the side of the cradle and the ladder. There are photographs which were taken to record the whole process.

The ambulance company, Aymed Emergencias Medicas, are friends now as we have become involved with many repatriations over the years. Always used by the private medical repatriation company, they are based in Tenerife and do a wonderful service. This was certainly one of their more unusual cases. The owners Antonio and Fabian could not believe Joanie's weight, which was around 230 kilos. During her stay in intensive care in reality she broke three beds until a more suitable substitute was found for her. "How is she going to get home" was Oscar's main worry. "She loves her own bed and familiar things" He told us countless times.

Now this time they were prepared for all eventualities. An air ambulance was, in due course, found who were equipped and prepared to carry Joanie and fly her home. Arriving on schedule Aymed picked them up from the airport. Everything had been thought of and the fire brigade was on stand by. Again, in cases which are uncommon, everything was being filmed for the record. Four ambulance men were on hand at the hospital and helped to slide Joanie from her bed into the ambulance. The mattress had been placed on the floor and off they went. Oscar was told to wait at the airport just in case there had been complications in moving her.

On arrival at the aircraft there were a second team of Aymed ambulance men waiting to help. She was expertly manoeuvred from the ambulance into the plane and onto a special mattress located also on the floor. The stretcher, normally used in these planes, was too high for Joanie to be positioned on. They finally took off and Joanie and Oscar were on their way home. She was admitted into the hospital near her home where she was stabilised sufficiently to be discharged. With Oscar by her side she was happier. He telephoned to give us an update for our records too. Thanks Oscar that tied off the ends nicely.

Another respiratory and very long case was Jake Miller. He came to us with an unexpected severe bout of bronchitis. Not really thinking he was so critical. He had been previously diagnosed with COPD which signifies chronic obstructive pulmonary disease. The holiday was turning into a nightmare for Jake and his wife Hilda. Several days had passed since he first felt that his condition was getting out of control. There was nothing else he could do but take the doctors advice and be admitted. He went straight onto 24 hour oxygen and strong medication to attempt to stabilise him. Lionel the lung specialist was pulling out all the stops. Jake was still insisting "I have to get home on my flight next week".

There were two similar cases in the room but the other gentleman was in the habit of treating himself. Jake was most confused but listened to Ralph as he went on and on about his infirmity. Ralph was writing everything down and then calling his own doctor at home for a second opinion. Poor Jake couldn't keep up. Ralph was removing his oxygen mask at every opportunity. "I'm having a try without to see how I get on". He would explain to Jake We reached the stage where quite honestly our Lionel was getting a bit angry. Trying to explain what was necessary and then turning our backs to find he was just doing "what my doctor at home told me but "was maddening.

The day dawned when we decided to give Ralph a change of accommodation and move him to a neighbouring room. This was good to start with until he began popping in to see Jake, "I want to see how he is doing", was Ralph's answer back. On request from Ralph's doctor, in the Uk that is, his medication was adjusted. Lionel did his best for him and he was able to be discharged. He went straight to the airport with a Mr Hugo to return on a flight with oxygen supplied specially for him. It was a case of "we did advise you about how you would be flying Ralph". Hope he is behaving himself and listening to his specialist.

Jake continued to stabilise very slowly but he complained of having a bad stomach. His condition was not improving as planned. The daily diet was altered to stop his severe diarrhoea. The antibiotic could have been causing it. But he wasn't improving and he was becoming weaker. Hilda was most concerned and moved into the hotel opposite the hospital. Their original flight came and went. His insurance was getting a day by day update of his situation. By now Jake couldn't get out of bed, least of all could he stand. The treating doctors, because there were now a lung specialist and a digestive specialist attending him, were baffled. As the days continued, Jake was forever positive but not improving quickly enough. The insurance decided to repatriate Jake and sent a nurse over. Not Mr Hugo again. On arriving at the hospital the medical situation was explained to her. By now our Lionel had made the decision that he was not well enough to travel.

When this happens all preparations are aborted and put on hold. The nurse escort was not happy to say the least. Making her calls to the insurance she tried hard to change Lionel's opinion. No go there as the decision was correct and based on Jakes medical condition. Lionel was the treating doctor and had the final word. He had taken a turn for the worse and had to be stabilised sufficiently again before being fit to fly. The next morning he moved into intensive care to have investigations for his present but out of the ordinary medical condition. The respiratory condition was proving very difficult and new tests were set up.

As the results began to appear he was diagnosed with a lung fungus. This was causing his situation but was treatable. First he was isolated and he began to improve slightly but was still very weak. Hilda was fantastic and an enormous help. Constantly at his side, when able, she encouraged Jake to eat a small but indicated diet. Between the doctors and the insurance company a repatriation plan by air ambulance was indicated. The day arrived for the air ambulance crew to be met at the airport. Their reaction on arrival was for the most part completely unexpected. The medical report in their possession was very different from the original requested by the insurance company. It did not mention his 'lung fungus' or that he was in isolation. They were not expecting a patient in his condition. After conversations with both our doctor and the insurance doctor it was decided to go ahead as Jakes isolation was only precautionary.

Hilda's face on leaving in the ambulance was a picture of happiness. Jake's I will never forget as he clutched my hand and looked deep into my eyes. He was going home even if it was via his local hospital. We received a call from their son a few days later and Jake was doing extremely well and starting to eat more solid foods. "He thanks you all from the bottom of his heart and God bless Lionel" was his emotional message. Jake, you were such a nice man and a pleasure to be able to help. I'm glad you passed our way and we sent you home.

Lung abscesses are not a regular condition seen in our hospital but Elton was an exception. Elton had arrived on holiday a few days earlier with his wife and daughter. "He has been losing weight for some time now" was the information given to us by his wife. He was not eating and felt very weak. On admittance he was not very well. Remember people on holiday will do anything not to admit that they really can't go on. Elton's daughter visited every day but was always late. She demanded to see Lionel out of visiting times. We had already done the rounds and given the update to Mildred, his wife. His daughter had many questions to ask and she admitted that she worked in a hospital. We never got to know exactly what her position was though.

Elton was not improving so between our specialist and the insurance company it was decided that he needed further extensive scans and a fibro scope. The process involves the following. A camera is inserted into his larynx and further into his bronchial tubes. The results would show if there was an obstruction and of what type. It could be a tumour or an abscess. Elton was getting rather depressed but the process was completed without delay. On receiving the results we spoke to Elton's wife and daughter alone. It was impossible to detect in which category the obstruction would be diagnosed. On discussion with his insurance it was decided to repatriate Elton with a doctor to complete the studies in Edinburgh.

We were sorry to see Elton leave as it was an undiagnosed condition for Lionel. He suspected that there was a tumour. The accompanying doctor was impressed with the organisation on our part. The conclusion of Elton's story is a happy one as we received information direct from the Lung Specialist in Edinburgh who was pleased to tell us that Elton's obstruction was in fact an abscess. I know Mildred and the whole family would have been overjoyed and very relieved with the news.

My last case to be mentioned in this chapter is a semi resident in the north of Mallorca. Gerald was such a private man that we kept him on his own in the room. He didn't get to converse with the only other British patient we originally moved in. On realising that he preferred to be alone we got the message. This was confirmed by his family. They were holidaying in their lovely villa on the north coast of Mallorca. It was really very nice, as I saw for myself one evening. That same night he was finally repatriated by Mr Hugo, I was invited by the family to locate the position for the ambulance company.

Gerald was initially a respiratory case but as we were stabilising him in this situation the circumstances changed. He was rather a severe case of cardiac insufficiency. In fact a walking time bomb! His pneumonia was treated without complications but on reviewing for his fit to fly it was decided he required a stress test. The Cardiologist was called and everything prepared for the process. How disappointing for the whole family when the results showed extensive heart damage. Gerald had had a previous heart attack some years before which had not been followed up or treated as was necessary. Finally the repatriation was set up and Gerald returned safely home to the Uk.

So many of these cases could have had a tragic ending. I have many more saved for the next book. The message, I hope, is becoming loud and clear. Remember any previous medical condition should and must be declared to the insurance. Please don't just take a free insurance offered by your travel agency. You don't want to end up as another patient "Watching the sun go down and the drip go up". Do you?

Chapter ten
LITTLE ONE'S PROBLEMS

Some of the more distressing times have been when children are admitted to the hospital. More so when the outcome is tragic. This does and can happen on numerous occasions. The families are absolutely distraught. Never in their wildest dreams would they imagine ending up in hospital with their child while on holiday. This is the moment when an interpreter's presence is most valuable. Many one parent families are holding everything together. If there is more than one child in the party "who will look after the others?" Again help is called upon from reps and tour operators. Until you unfortunately find yourself involved in a situation like this you cannot imagine the distress.

Children are most generally admitted with acute gastroenteritis. They are treated and discharged in a short time. This is kinder as they will invariably be able to continue their holiday without delay. Mothers are distraught when they are told that" little one must stay with us". The family is given their own room as here in Spain a child under fifteen has to be accompanied by an adult. They cannot be left alone over night. Treatment is rapidly put into action and improvement is rapidly seen to be happening. Smiles are back on their faces within a very short time.

Normally with gastroenteritis cases twenty four to forty eight hours is sufficient to get a patient back on track. The drip goes up to rehydrate immediately, nil by mouth ordered and we wait. When the treating doctor advises that the patient can start on a diet it doesn't mean that the parent can go out and get a 'burger' for the patient. I can recall going into a room after the doctor had done his round to find that Dad had brought some food in. "The doctor said he could start eating" was Dad's reply. "Yes, he can but only what the doctor has ordered" was my answer to that. Understandably the patient is desperately hungry but a solid diet is introduced gradually. They try liquids first which could be apple juice, progressing onto more solid astringent foods. When the patient is tolerating this diet adequately we can begin to consider an imminent discharge. The family can then get on with the fun.

During the summer months we have numerous cases of chicken pox. Frequently the child has been in contact with other children at nursery. "I'm sure chicken pox was going around" Mum will tell us. A child will not be declared fit to fly until all the spots are almost invisible. If they tried to get on a flight they would be turned away. Through the air conditioning in the plane the chicken pox bug will travel. Many months later a tour company could be facing heavy claims. Imagine if a newly pregnant woman was sitting near and remembered the child who had lots of spots. What if the old lady travelling developed shingles? All part of the chicken pox family I'm afraid.

The family is normally told to separate. The insurance will only pay for one person to remain with the patient when their customer misses their original flight due to similar circumstances. Many times though I have found that Mum or Dad will not return and leave the rest of the family behind. They are advised that they must pay the additional costs. When flying home together the third party will be required to pay the going price for their seat. This can be very expensive. My help is valuable to find and secure the best practical situation for the family Extended accommodation can be found in an apartment so the insurance will be paying for this unit. We get away with hiding the extra cost for these family members.

The child will be required to see the doctor again for a fit to fly certificate. Only then will the insurance look to repatriate and get them home. The added upsetting part for the family is that they cannot swim in the hotel's swimming pool at all. They almost have to be kept out of sight with some severe cases.. But all ends well and they get home as soon as is possible. Not a very pleasant way to have an extra few days holiday.

A child can develop an acute appendicitis at any time; this is devastating while on holiday. But happens time and again. An emergency operation is called for, performed and then the wait begins. If it occurs at the beginning of the holiday they may be in time for their original flight. A patient must not fly for up to ten days after an operation. I can remember one patient's Dad holding parties while waiting for the time to go home. I was asked to bring the biscuits and drinks once. The "patients" were waiting on the balcony to see if I had remembered when I came on duty. After a week of partying and a fit to fly certificate signed Alan and his Dad were allowed to get back to their life. I think they really missed us and the experience was something they will not forget in a hurry. Dad considered it would be a good tale to tell at family gatherings.

Tonsillitis and ear infections are very common with children after flying abroad on holiday. Days spent immersed in the swimming pool's water can cause an inner ear infection. This will stop them from flying home as the air pressure could permanently damage their eardrums. No fit to fly certificate will be issued until the doctor is satisfied that they are fit. Invariably they will be delayed and fly home only days later. But they get home safely with no further damage. The trauma of being separated is soon forgotten.

Everyone deserves a holiday including pregnant women. Numerous patients have "lost their baby while on holiday". It is so sad to have to inform a lady in the early stage of pregnancy that a D&C has to be performed. In many occasions this occurs around three months. Whether it is the flying which could have caused this or the hot sun is a mystery. Insurance Companies consider it safe for a pregnant woman to fly up to twenty eight weeks but each case is really individual. A letter from the patient's doctor is also recommended. Their partners attempt to console them as is best possible. They return home to "try again".

In the hospital we have recorded quite a number of cases where the pregnancy is considerably advanced. Babies have been prematurely born on countless occasions. Little Melanie was one of these babies. She had been a twin but the other baby died and was still born. Melanie fought so hard and lived. She spent the first three months of her life in our hospital going from strength to strength. The nurses would bring in dolls clothes as she progressed. Melanie's Mum and Dad were very young but tremendous in their concern for their little girl. Visits from family members who came and went but meanwhile as they described "our miracle baby" fought on.

She had to gain a lot of weight before they could consider her fit to fly. Melanie made it and eventually returned home without a Spanish accent though as she wasn't up to a talking stage when she left us. Her Mum and Dad were so proud of their little Spanish daughter. They have an unaccountable number of photos to show her as she gets older. What an experience for them. This was only made possible with the support both from their insurance company and devoted family members.

Sometimes the situation can occur at a time when it is not really possible for the baby to survive. Little 'Jack' was only at a twenty three week stage when he came into the world very unexpectedly. His Mum was in labour for two days before he finally arrived. While there is a heartbeat showing on the machines we just have to wait. We are in Spain so this is normal practice. The doctors had already informed the new parents that there was no chance the baby would survive. To Mum and Dad this baby was real and they wanted to be able to deal with everything as it should be.

By contacting the consulate and the funeral parlour we arranged that Mum would be with her baby for as long as was possible. The birth happened during the night. How wonderful for them that we had everything under control. Little 'Jack' came into the world in a foreign country but unfortunately only lived for five hours. He was cradled in Mum and Dad's arms during his short existence. When the time came and he passed away they were at peace with the situation. He was repatriated very quickly and had a funeral with all the family present. A couple of months later we received a letter from them. It was thanking us for our help. Inside the card were Jack's hand and footprints taken especially for his remembrance card. I was greatly moved but felt glad to have made a difference to them all.

These cases are unusual but you never know what is coming next. Little ones have accidents too and are very vulnerable while in hospital "on their hols". Some cases have been mentioned in the chapter on fractures. Everyone is at risk and should always be careful. Little ones need looking after and guided through their foreign holiday. They are more distressed than adults as it is strange for them with the language. Our Paediatricians are first class and wonderful with children.

Young Robert was a live wire and his family lovely. They had to be separated so off to the airport went Robert's Mum and sister. We nearly had another patient on our hands as Mum complained of pain before she was due to leave the hospital. A quick examination in A&E declared her fit to fly. Robert's complaint was also a deep ear infection.

The two men, son and father, spent their extra time in the hospital waiting for tests to be done. They were so desperate to return home but had to be uncomplaining. The time came for the final check up. Dad was already on the laptop looking for flights. Eventually the insurance agreed that Dad could book flights quicker than their travel department. They collected their things and were ready to go in record time.

Robert was being very secretive until I coaxed from him that he had had a dream where the man in the room next door was fighting for his life with a heart attack. Suddenly from the radio a well known song was played. Robert thought it a good omen and extremely funny that the song was ´Staying alive ´ by the Bee Gees. Everyone was overjoyed and surprised when the man in the next room survived a massive heart attack some three hours later.

Maybe children are psychic, who can dispute that fact. I wouldn't like to try,

When a semi drowning occurs the potentially fatal situation is disturbing. Three year old Joseph was on holiday with Grandma. While she was attending the welcome meeting Joseph slipped away unnoticed to take a look at the swimming pool. Without delay he was located as Grandma acted immediately. He had removed his T-shirt and jumped into the shallow end of the pool. Luckily he had been swallowing water for a very short time. This was enough for him to become unconscious. He was pulled from the water and given mouth to mouth by the lifeguard while waiting for the ambulance to arrive. Joseph was in a coma when admitted to the hospital but everything was being done for him.

Grandma was distraught as she had also had to contact her daughter at home. She couldn't believe how quickly Joe had slipped out. An all night vigil was rewarded within a short time. Children are extremely resilient and come bouncing back very rapidly. Grandma was waiting for her daughter who was flying out within hours. When Joe's mum arrived Grandma was able to give her the good news that he was out of danger. The risk of infection through the lungs has to be controlled. It isn't normal for water to be in the lungs and infection can occur very quickly. Joe stayed with us for a couple of days but was none the worse for wear after his experience.

As a team we have to sort out numerous cases of children admitted to the hospital. A special attention is given to the families often with short regular visits from one or all of us during our shifts. The whole family is in need of that bit extra and an explanation from the doctor is sometimes not enough. A lot of reassurance makes a dreadful situation bearable for them all. It is extremely disheartening for Mums and Dads to have to wait for their discharge papers once the doctor has told them that the child is fit to leave hospital. The doctor is really declaring them fit to continue the holiday and fit to fly home. This is without doubt, essential for the airline company. Though even more important for the tour operator.

Our doctors will discharge children just a soon as they can. One very anxious Mum was so keen to get moving that when I said that the doctor gave his permission for them to leave the room and walk around the roundabout a bit. This is exactly what she did. Our hospital is cross shaped with four corridors meeting at the centre to form a round distribution area.

Two hours later we found the patient and family entering the main door. We quickly stopped the little group to determine if they had been out of the hospital. The answer they gave me still makes me chuckle. "Yes we have, what a nice doctor to let us get some fresh air. We've been to the roundabout." They'd been to the big roundabout on the main road! To get there you have to follow a short path, go over a bridge and mingle through the traffic.

The said roundabout can be seen from the hospital and looks very pretty with palm trees in the centre. There is an old nightclub building to the side. They also fed the ducks as their little party crossed the bridge. The doctor had referred to where the corridors on their floor in the of the hospital meet. We all identify it as the roundabout. Think their roundabout was more appealing than ours!

Little Lucas was admitted on his last day so inevitably he missed his original flight. Mum was with him constantly. His auntie would not think of leaving them. Lucky lady worked for British Airways so using all her organising skills she arranged to stay with the little family. Lucas now had two "Mums". During the first few hours Lucas seemed to improve but gradually the doctors realised that this wasn't a normal case of gastroenteritis. The indicated treatment wasn't having the desired effect.

Further advice and tests were underway. The insurance company were adamant they would not pay for all the occupants of the hospital room. We have family rooms which are big enough. With a put up bed added are sufficient for a family. After a couple of days we diagnosed little Lucas with Mononucleosis. His mum was shocked but everything was fully explained to her. A few days later they were ready to go home. Auntie organising them all or so she thought. She didn't take into consideration the insurance company's opinion though. However all ended well as they left our care on way to the airport all together and on the same flight too.

Accidents will occur on holiday but when children are involved it becomes even more distressing. Watching them during the twenty four hours in a day cannot avoid this happening. Eyes in the back of your head will not stop the situation. So remember if you do get into this circumstance you will have the backing of interpreters and a good insurance I'm sure. Just let the right people help and assist you. The assistance given is already tried and tested. We won't fail you. But we'll still hold your hand while "you watch the sun go down and the drip go up"

Chapter eleven
A WEE DROP TOO MUCH

A holiday is waited for with considerable anticipation. It is the highlight of the year for most travellers. A years saving and planning results in euphoria unknown with other events. After fifty weeks you are off. New clothes and excitement are in the suitcase. The holiday starts at the airport for many with the remark "Let's have a drink before our flight" This can result in some tourist being refused boarding due to alcohol excess. The majority take their flight and start to enjoy being abroad. The drinks in most foreign countries are considerably stronger than at home. Unfortunately this is badly handled by some. The results of a wee drop too much is following so read on and be aware of what can occur.

Roger, who was two months off 18, was holidaying with three friends. Because of his age and it was the first holiday away, his parents wanted to keep an eye on them. They booked into the hotel next door. Imagine their shock when they were informed that he was in hospital. Roger was admitted with five stomach ulcers. He'd had to have a gastro scope. And what a shock to see the photos! Apparently, and heed this warning. If you are knocking back shots all night, you need to eat too! Roger and his pals drank all night and slept all day. Leaving no time for eating. Consequently removing the lining of his stomach in the process. His Dad was more than surprised might I add.

The family recovered from their shock but took control. Roger was treated for his condition. If the ulcer had been left much longer it could have ruptured. The consequences would have been a great deal more serious. In this case Roger was lucky that Dad was on hand to come to his rescue. 'The boys' do not eagerly call a doctor and hope the symptoms will quickly fade away. When the patient is finally seen it is evident that considerable time has passed. Maybe they hadn't even thought of their insurance. Maybe they didn't even have one! The excess, to be paid, seems unnecessary to them. They would rather have a couple more drinks. Don't let this happen to you.

Poor Anna may still have the scars to show for her holiday dare. 'Oso Bucos' games were being played. These are 'shots' which you set alight. A hand swiftly darts across the glass to put out the flame. Immediately you 'knock back' the shot. The degree of alcohol has been increased. Anna hadn't done this before. The glass went to her lips and she poured flaming alcohol around her mouth, chin and over her T shirt. Her face, hands ,chest and her neck caught alight! Mum arrived to help and comfort her. She was distraught at the state of her daughter. "What on earth possesses these people to try such games on young vulnerable people" she cried "It should be illegal" "It happens so quickly and just goes wrong" I comforted her. There is no way we can stop these games and they will continue. The holiday makers are out for a good time. The burns she had were treated during the week she spent with us. She was Ok but I don't think she will try that again.

Frequently our team exchange experiences when we have had a holiday ourselves or taken some time off. One of the subjects commonly talked about is 'the wee drop too much' that the Brits seem to take as natural while away from home. It is their holiday after all. The local onlookers think it funny and accepted to see customers appearing legless and undeniably over the limit. Once this situation becomes out of hand or dangerous then it changes everything. This is when accidents happen and the revellers end up in our care.

As I have said throughout the book an emergency can occur at any moment so we always have to be prepared. While visiting my favourite bar in Tenerife called Mary Rogan's, I was called upon to assist an English gentleman. I have been visiting this same bar for about five years and can go there alone without feeling conspicuous. The owners, Colette and Michael have become friends. There was a commotion outside as Michael was singing 'Forty shades of green'. A man had collapsed! Michael stopped his show of course. Because he knows what work I do he asked me to "hold the man's hand until the ambulance gets here". The man could have had a stroke or a heart attack. It was potentially a serious situation.

The Aymed ambulance arrived in record time. On seeing me they were surprised but acted quickly. The patient, English of course, was taken off to the local hospital. The show continued but everyone had had rather a shock. Knowing one and all were rather alarmed and anxious Fabian, the ambulance man, telephoned me about two hours later to advise that the man was under observation. A heart attack had been ruled out, a stroke too. Even though pending further tests he was going to be alright. The atmosphere visibly relaxed and the show proceeded.

The police have their time taken up with balcony cases in the busy summer months. Mickie was just one of the luckier ones. There are always too many balcony falls every season but this day there were four such cases recorded. Unfortunately the other three had fatal endings but Mickie's fall was broken by a window ledge on the second floor. He sustained multiple fractures in his leg and severe bruising in his back. The internal conditions were however treatable Taken straight into intensive care as arrangements were being made and his parents were informed. He then went onto treatment which saved his life. Mickie had suffered dreadful shock when he realised just how lucky he had been. He sobered up instantly but of course the police knew he was another crazy tourist.

Mickie recovered satisfactorily and was given orders that he could be repatriated. The hospital gave him information but no help. As mentioned he was in an NHS hospital so no help was available from the NHS for repatriation. Mr Hugo was contacted and arranged his safe transfer home in record time. Mickie was very embarrassed but took everything well. His uncle had paid for his repatriation and demanded that common sense should exist for the future. This is not on sale but we know that he learnt a significant lesson from his experience. Mr Hugo helped him to see how his thoughtless attitude had paid off.

Understandably there is always a certain amount of

alcohol abuse with most of these cases. It will show in their blood stream and will have to be disclosed on the medical report. The circumstances can and do happen in all categories of our visiting tourists. A young thirty year old was on holiday with her three year old son and a girlfriend. Carol and Alice had been drinking most of the evening in a popular bar near the hotel. Around one o'clock it was time to call it a day so back to the hotel they headed. On arrival in their room the friends went onto the balcony. In no time Carol fell deeply asleep on a chair but Alice took the child to bed where she also curled up and slept.

An hour later she was woken by a heavy banging on the door. It was the police inquiring how many occupants there were to the room. "Are you all here?" was the policeman's question. Alice replied that they were. She quickly went to wake Carol so she would be more comfortable in her bed. On finding the terrace empty she thought Carol was in the bathroom. But no! Carol, on waking had intended to go to bed so stood up and turned to enter the room. She was still very drunk and turned the wrong way. Like a rag doll she had gone over the balcony.

The police had been called as some guests had witnessed the event. It was a forth floor balcony and was fatal for Carol. Alice had no choice but to take charge and full control of the little boy. An emergency passport was obtained and permission for Alice to travel home as quickly as was possible. After identifying her friend she wanted to get home and sort things from there. The help given to her was amazing and she was accompanied to the airport without delay by her tour operator. She was not alone for a moment and crisis psychologists were on hand.

We heard no more about this distressing balcony case but hope it is not repeated again. Young and old are not aware of the very real dangers when your guard is down and you are enjoying yourselves having a bit of fun. "We are on holiday after all" is the common reply. Don't let it get out of hand though so enjoy your well earned holiday of a lifetime. Make sure you want to and can return the following year.

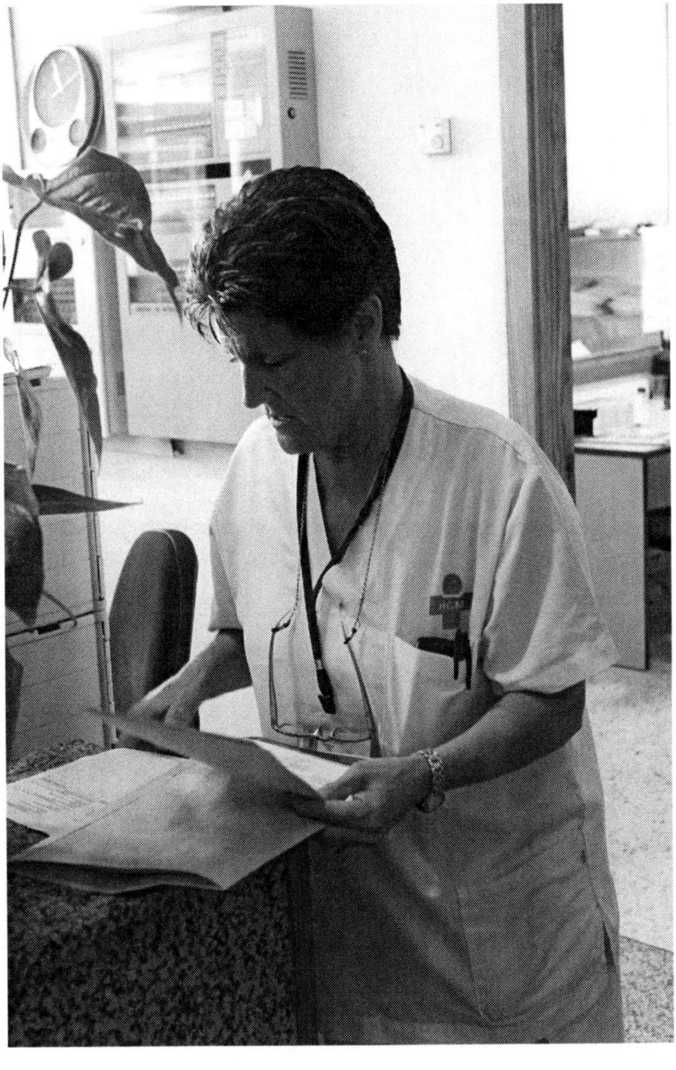

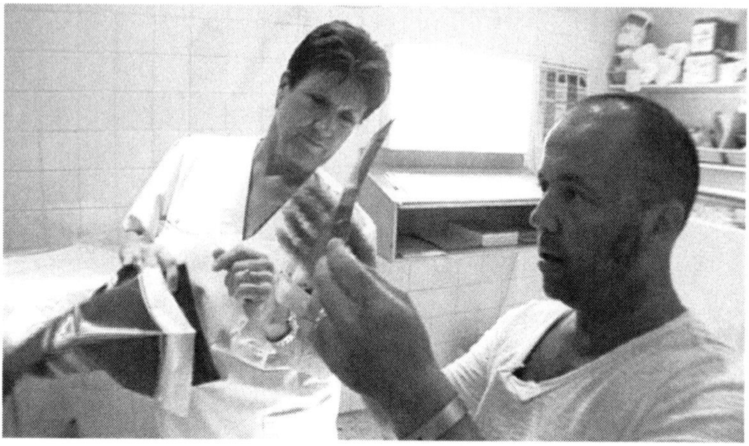

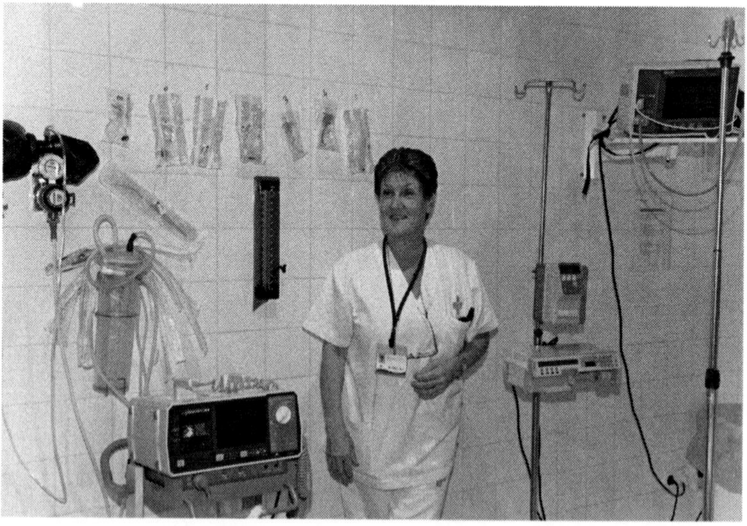

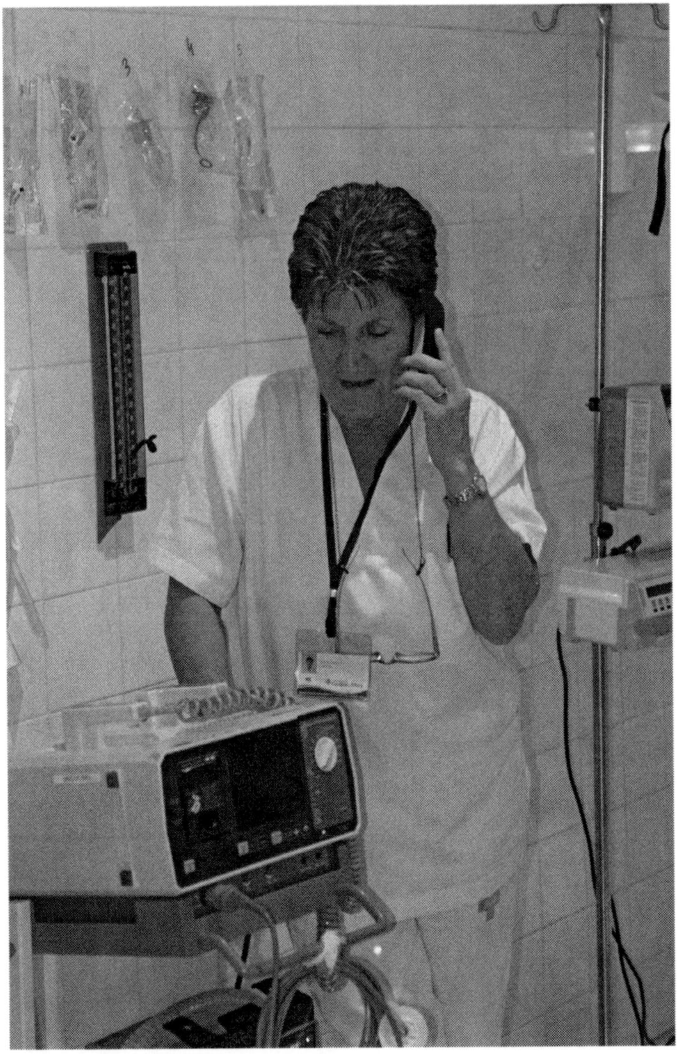

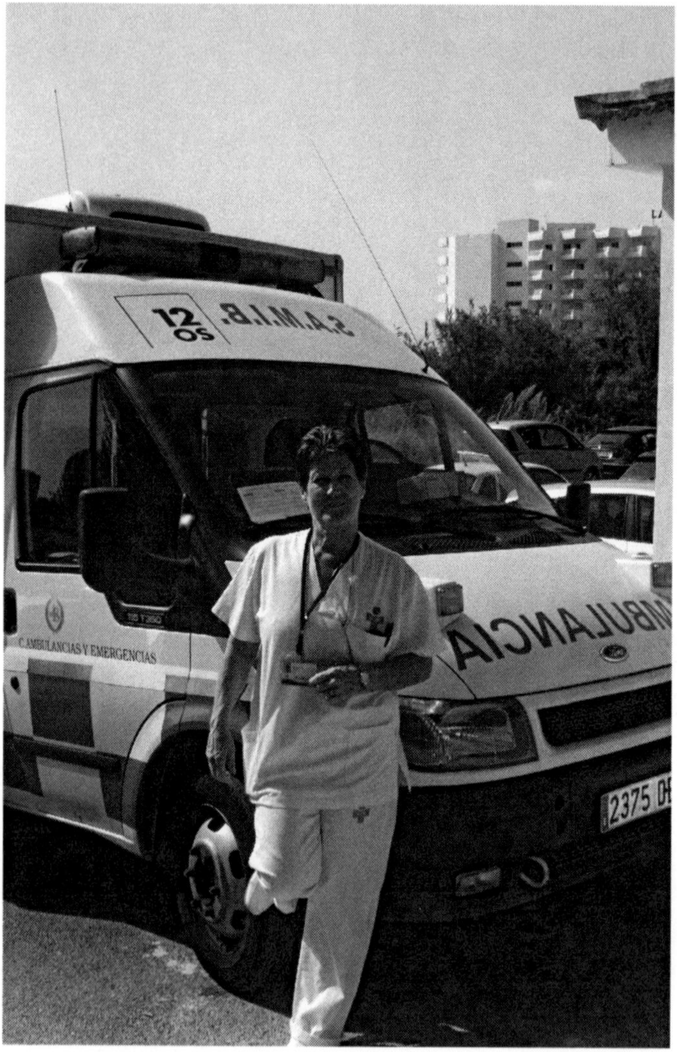
C.AMBULANCIAS Y EMERGENCIAS

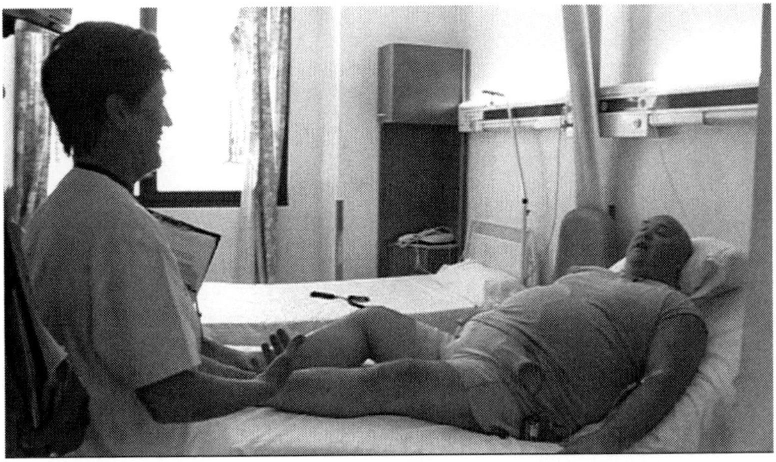

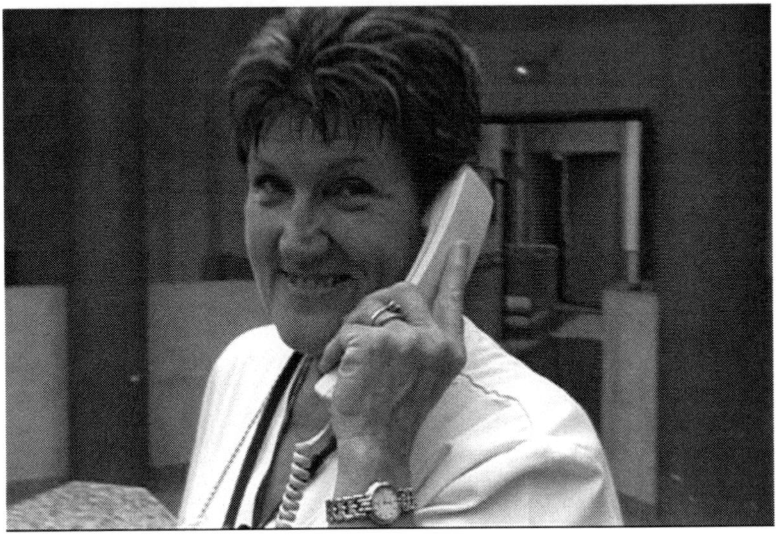

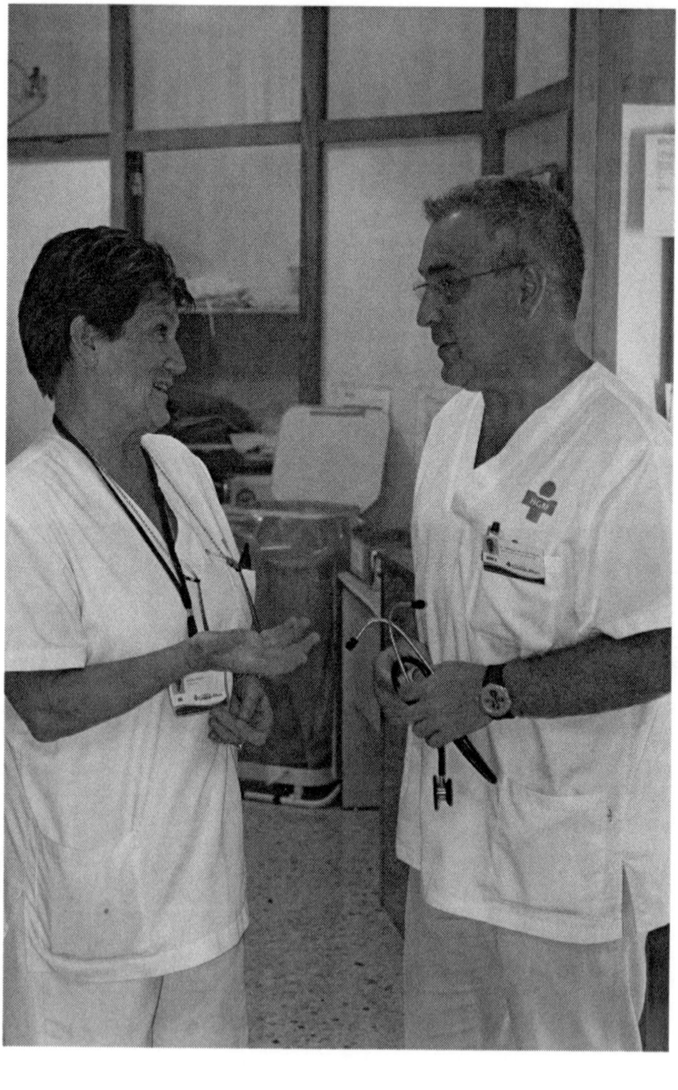

Chapter 12
SUN, SEA AND A&E

We are now coming to the end of my first book with only some of the memorable cases over the last decade. Let's hope the message has been spotted and observed loud and clear. When you next go on holiday I trust that you will have really looked into your holiday insurance. Will you insure you have adequate cover?

Last summer we were approached by a film company who wished to spend some time in our hospital filming the British who find themselves "watching the sun go down and the drip go up". They too wanted to get the message across.

The series produced was called 'Sun, Sea and A&E' and has now been aired for the third time and given credibility to the cases which occurred during the busy summer season. I have been recording my work from over a decade and I felt sure one day that it would all go down on paper. I needed to get the message across in the hope it would save a lot of heartache and distress for some families. However it is too late for the families I have already been involved with. But the series has given me the opportunity to warn holidaymakers in the future as it has been watched by over two million people.

Suzanne and Lucy arrived to have a chat one day. Little did I know that they were actually the producers. We exchanged ideas and obtained written permission for them to come into the hospital. Plans were put into action and off they went. The filming, which was reasonably unobtrusive took form and our patients got to tell their stories when asked. The crew spent about six weeks collecting information with us. Some very interesting cases were put on tape. You may have watched them over the eight weeks in which Sun, Sea and A&E was aired. Don't be disappointed if you missed the first series as a second has been already agreed.

As an interpreter you come across many mentionable situations. Things are said which come out wrong when you are stressed and pushed to the limit. My colleagues have many memories too. When I first started translating it was with a friend called Michelle. She introduced me to all the little 'hiccups'. These are so numerous that we would need another book to tell them all. I was so keen to learn but my attention was caught by some expressions which can be misinterpreted. These are never recorded for publication though.

Michelle reiterated time and time again that "Patients are never patient". They want and need to know all the ins and outs. They think we know everything. Rushing around trying to get patients discharged as quickly as possible. "We are on holiday you know" is said so many times with a bit of ungratefulness thrown in. Finally we got information for one patient who was practically out of the door before we knew. He was to be repatriated the following morning. This was all he wanted to know but his wife was more inquisitive." Don't you worry about a thing" Michelle assured them. But they were already mentally at the airport.

We all have funny stories to tell each other after a days interpreting. Just recently the team had a few laughs over some ways that certain advice and information is given. Most of the doctors who work with us do speak quite a lot of English. Some of them believe they make themselves clearly understood not misunderstood. Not always the case unfortunately.

Harold had had his operation. All had gone to plan and he was waiting to go home. Dr House had been to see about discharging him. All agreed and we were just waiting for his medical report. On re visiting him he informed me that a seat was going to be taken out of the plane so he could fly. Now that's very strange and not usual practice. I expressed the idea that "Maybe you've got it wrong?"

Harold was adamant that this is what Dr House had said. After a little more probing I realised that the doctor had actually told the patient apparently that an extra seat had to be taken out in the plane for his leg to be elevated. It must be confusing for the proud doctor to comprehend that taking out another seat is said in the following way. "When reserving your flight the insurance company should make sure they book an extra seat for you". Harold was most disturbed and was imagining seeing the mechanics using screwdrivers to remove a seat specially for his leg. The lady in the next room had also been caught in conversation as to how this would be carried out. Harold expressively told her "That's definitely what the doctor said"

How can you translate some expressions which we

use consistently? For example how can a Spanish speaker understand "He's pulling your leg" There is a similar expression used by the Spanish which translated literally means. "Hes taken (cut) your hair. Doesn't make sense does it? With another doctor, during translation, I added that there were no medals for running before you can walk. It took me a while to explain to him but he understood. I hadn't translated what he had said you see!

The film crew was also keen to feature some of the holiday reps who were ill while working here. The roles change places and they get a taste of what it is realistically like for their customers. One new rep was admitted to hospital with very deep cut on her instep. She had been partying all night and ended up in a bar where they were to have the last one. When talking to her that morning I discovered that she couldn't remember how many vodka and red bulls she had consumed the previous night. On recounting we chalked up eleven! Now eleven drinks of this nature are unthinkable in her home town so imagine how strong they must have been. She couldn't remember a thing and certainly not the pain. "I just saw a lot of blood" she cried to me. Her scar for the nine stitches is still visible today. She won't forget her season as a rep.

During the summer season most reps will need to recharge their batteries so when a rep ends up in hospital with gastroenteritis we put them in the category of 'your time to recharge your batteries so make the most of it' They can and are admitted for many medical conditions though. We hope they are none the worse for the experience. Maybe they are more sympathetic with their customers who find themselves hospitalised too. Any support given by the 'friendly rep' is welcome and invaluable. They should be there to help and advise, listen and observe.

While we also look after our VIPs, who are the reps, there can also be very strange phenomenon occurring to them while working away from home. One very bizarre case was the following rather distressing clinical situation. Something that a rep could never imagine happening to her in this case came true. Nicky had been rushed into A&E with severe stomach pains and bleeding we were amazed to find on examination that she had a tumour on her ovary.

An operation was required immediately. The difficulty for us as translators arose when she had to be informed of the nature of the tumour. It was impossible to repeat word for word what the Gynaecologist was saying. Our team has an extremely good relationship with all the doctors but how can you tell a young girl of twenty three years old that the tumour contains hair and teeth! Nicky would immediately think she had had an ectopic pregnancy. Although it is a fairly common type of tumour it conjures up unimaginable pictures. The tumour is formed when three layers of developing tissues become tangled and do not separate as normal.

The doctor agreed with me after I had explained in my own words the situation and the need for an operation. Her parents arrived without delay and were at her side during her stay with us. She had been lucky as the tumour was on the point of rupturing and had already stated leaking and causing slight peritonitis. Peritonitis, if left, can be very serious indeed.

One very friendly rep always told us she imagined that the people involved could be her direct family. "How would they manage and what help would they have?" she exclaimed!

Putting herself in this position really helped her to cope with the more serious ones." If my Mum was ill what would her rep do for her?" She asked herself constantly. Another mum arrived on the first obtainable flight when her daughter called to say she had been admitted to hospital with a reoccurrence of her asthma. She was so grateful for the help and attention given by her daughter's fellow reps. "If they are as good with their customers as with my daughter they need medals" Mum informed us.

Sun, Sea and A&E were flies on the wall during the filming and between us maybe the message has been heeded and observed. They too were astounded by the unthought-of occurrences during your holiday. The unforeseen will happen again and again. Suzanne and Lucy have become firm friends after we shared some of the funny, sad and heart rending cases they filmed while peeping at the holidaymakers. General expectations for your holiday don't include a visit to A&E but if it does maybe you will meet me or someone in the same role. You could feature in the next series of Sun, Sea and A&E already underway. We'll hold your hand and be there to advise and help. We'll watch too as "The sun goes down and the drip goes up".

As the summer draws to an end and the holiday season closes all the memories will fade slightly. Next year is another story though. Could you be featured in the next series or the next instalment of my book? Take care and remember to scrutinise your insurance in detail. Declare everything and anything you can think of. Even if the travel agent tells you it is not necessary. Insist that you want that in writing too. Think of how many times you have taken out a travel insurance and never needed it. One day you may be one of the unlucky who find that they have to see a doctor while on holiday. No matter how simple your ailments make sure you declare it. It will be worth it in the end.

Not all cases end as we would like unfortunately. We will constantly see patients in the hospital who have had a ´change of accommodation´ while on holiday. Our team will always be on hand to help with kind words and a lot of tender loving care. I am content to have been there for them and been able to help. You may have seen the end result and "Sun, Sea and A&E" on TV recently. If you did see the programme lets hope you have enjoyed reading about them too in this book. Take note that "When the sun goes down and the drip goes up" these holidaymakers need all the assistance possible.

HAPPY HOLIDAY.

About the Author

Gill Bucklitsch was born in Bristol but moved to Majorca over thirty years ago. She married a local man and has five grown up children. She devoted her early married life combining bringing up her children and teaching her native language. Returning to work twelve years ago she looked after the welfare of hospitalised customers for MyTravel. Being a dormant career woman she found immense job satisfaction and started to make notes on numerous cases over a decade.

Moving from MyTravel two years ago, after the merger with another tour operator, she joined the welfare team as an interpreter in a hospital in the north of Majorca.

Then followed the filming of Sun, Sea and A&E which motivated her to complete her first book of her experiences while translating for the "Brits" She feels she has a message for all of you.